400 MORE
CREATIVE WAYS
TO SAY
I LOVE YOU

D0826921

400 More Creative Ways to Say I Love You

ALICE CHAPIN

Living Books®
Tyndale House Publishers, Inc.
Wheaton, Illinois

The compiler and editors have taken reasonable care to trace ownership and, when necessary, to obtain permission for each selection
included. If any questions of ownership arise, corrections will be made
in subsequent printings.

Printed in the United States of America

01 00 99 98 97 96
7   6   5   4   3   2   1

A Word from the Author

I shudder to think anybody would use this book for simple solutions to serious marriage problems. Rather, it is a collection of bright ideas and creative suggestions that can stoke the fires of romance. They are offered by the world's best lovers, common-sense men and women of all ages and from all walks of life whose marriages seem to be surviving and thriving. Nobody claims that these are perfect couples, but since they have found ways to hang together through good and bad, amidst the hectic pace of two-career families and the discouragement of rising divorce statistics, their secrets deserve to be heard. Every idea won't suit every couple, but some of these suggestions just might send your own love life back into orbit.

I met these couples everywhere—on seashore vacations, on airplanes, in seminars and discussion groups or retreats that I conducted. A few wise pastors and long-time counselors, as well as friends, acquaintances, and relatives also shared their wisdom. It was high time someone asked these savvy experts to emerge from the peaceful seclusion of their happy homes to share "inside stuff" from their lives. Almost all of them felt flattered. A few exclaimed, "We thought you'd never ask!" After *400 Ways to Say "I Love You"* was published, many new ideas were volunteered by appreciative readers who wrote letters and made phone calls from all over the map. Perhaps as you try out some of these ways to show love, you will come to the same conclusion I did: Experience definitely counts!

One woman told me, "Most couples desire to love better, but don't know how. From time to time we all do small things to show we care, but many of us just muddle along because that is all we know. We need new and better ways to play this old game." That is why I put this book together.

These idea starters span the range of sentimental, serious, personal, and very meaningful expressions of love. Many are giddy and raucous, silly and lighthearted enough to evoke giggles and belly laughs (after all, what connects a couple better than fun?). Others are richly romantic, tender, even sensuous. None are copyrighted. You can actually use them without penalty to see if they work in your own life!

A word to the wise: Giving away love in new ways carries a risk. The recipient may not feel as comfortable as you with new happenings. That shouldn't stop you! Don't force your ideas, but don't let anything hold you back either! These are secrets that have made other good marriages even better, so why not yours? If one suggestion doesn't work, try another. Then another. Be patient. And don't be hindered by quaint ideas about your age or the importance of a price tag.

Attitude is everything, especially if resentment rears its ugly thoughts inside your head just because your partner seldom seems willing to launch anything new. Being the one who initiates caring gestures does not make you a martyr. Bringing creativity to a relationship is a privilege. Just jump the attitude hurdle and remind yourself that you are building a relationship, not sacrificing yourself. You are a willing giver of love who expects nothing in return (although up ahead you will likely reap the good results). Your partner may even find some of these ideas so exciting that he or she will eventually try a few. Didn't the Master of Love say, "Love never fails"?

Each day has 1440 minutes. Maybe you could set aside just five of them to make time for some brand-new little or large labor of love that will nurture your relationship.

FOR MEN ONLY: This book is a two-for-one special. I have addressed it to women primarily. But you good guys out there are allowed to peek into these pages; it can become an everyMAN'S guide when ideas are applied in reverse. So, go ahead, take a closer look, then scribble a few of these marriage builders down on your calendar. A good marriage is a terrible thing to waste.

Contents

Love Spoken Here
The language of love for tongue-tied lovers

Gentle words cause life and health.

PROVERBS 15:4

Love expressed is love enhanced. Sweet somethings, spoken or written, are an infinitely valuable gift to your partner and must be expressed. "I love you" can (and should) be said in a thousand different ways to add spice to the message. Men and women alike never grow tired of hearing it, because each time the words send shafts of warmth into yearning hearts. A few magic phrases that express true heartfelt feelings can be instant therapy for a relationship in the doldrums and are a necessity for good marriage maintenance.

1

Sweet talk, seasoned to taste, spoken or written, can pop up anywhere, anytime, and will make you feel good, too. If you consider yourself a little tongue-tied, here is a big supply of love lines masterminded by caring couples just like you.

- I want what's best for you.
- I want you to be happy.
- You light up my life.
- I like belonging to you.
- I love you better than anybody.
- I wouldn't last a week without you.
- You're the best of all.
- My love for you is stronger than this problem. We'll get through it.
- You have good thoughts and ideas.
- We make a pretty good team.
- You've given me the best years of my life by giving me the best years of yours.
- Nobody does it better.
- I love you today, too.
- I love being yours.
- God blessed me with you.
- You're wonderful!
- You're good for me.
- I love the way you make me feel.

- Thanks for putting up with all my little quirks all these years.
- You are the husband I always wanted.
- You fill my gaps.
- How do you expect me to remember your birthday when you never look any older?
- Our love grows better every year.
- You're my quiet refuge.
- I love to hear the doorknob turn at 5:30. I know it's you.
- I'm glad you're home.
- I'm having a wonderful time being married.
- I thanked God for you today.
- I wouldn't trade you for anybody.
- I'd marry you all over again.
- Remember how we felt when they played our favorite song? I still feel that way.
- I love you more now than when I married you.
- Happiness is being married to your best friend. You are mine.
- You are everything I ever wanted in a husband.
- You are even better than I dreamed.
- Our love was meant to be.

- God must have loved me a lot to bless me with you.
- You're wonderful to me.
- I love you because you love God. That makes all the difference.
- You're a winner. I hit the jackpot when I got you.
- I will think about what you said. You may be right.
- Thank you.
- Thank you for allowing me to be angry and disappointed. I needed to get it all out.
- I believe in us.
- I'm sorry. I was wrong.
- I'm trying hard to understand things from your point of view.
- Knowing you love me cheers me up when I'm blue.
- You spice up my life.
- What are you doing New Year's?

❀ ❀ ❀

How to say "I love you" in other languages:

- Hawaiian: Aloha wau ia oe
- Italian: Ti amo
- Spanish: Te amo
- French: Je t'aime

- Russian: Ya lyubluy tyebya
- Greek: S'agapo

THE WRITE STUFF

More than kisses, letters mingle souls.

JOHN DONNE

"Me? Write my mate a love letter after all these years?" Feeling awkward? Just write the letter anyway! Your marriage matters. Sometimes written is easier than spoken. If one of you died tomorrow, would you have regrets about things unsaid? Most of us would.

Love lines don't need to be letter-perfect. Just be yourself. Make your sentimental message long or short, prose or poetry, serious or lighthearted, maybe wonderfully wacky but tenderhearted just like the two of you, or whatever else fits your style. Jazz it up with computer graphics if you wish. Write your sweet message on plain white typing paper or make it come alive with your color of choice. Whatever you do, your caring words will be savored, then saved to be read over and over.

❀ ❀ ❀

Make your sweetie's heart skip a beat by leaving your written expression of love in a book he is reading, or stick your letter in his briefcase or leave it on his pillow sometime when you will be away for the night.

❀ ❀ ❀

High-tech gadgets can lend a hand, too, so fax your mild or wild words or scrawl them on the overhead projector he uses on the job (take care who's around the next time he turns it on!).

❀ ❀ ❀

I know a woman who purposefully hid her love letter in the freezer. Wednesday is her husband's television night, and she knew that he would go for ice during commercial breaks when the midevening munchies set in. Finding the letter, he abandoned his easy chair and slipped away to his office to read her note privately.

❀ ❀ ❀

If you decide to mail your love letter, you can put the stamp on upside down (you know what that means, don't you?), and of course you would select the special love stamp available at the post office. How about mailing your letter to him from the hometown as a surprise from you while you are away visiting your parents?

❋ ❋ ❋

You can write your love message:

- on the outside of a big balloon, or stuff your letter inside a clear balloon
- in the dust atop the bedroom dresser or piano
- in the sand at the seashore
- on a billboard you rent
- on the inside bottom of a lunch box or tackle box
- on Post-it notes you've left everywhere around the house. Stick one to the sandwich in his briefcase, on the coffeepot or his favorite mug, in his medicine cabinet, on his aftershave bottle, in the pocket of a shirt or jacket he will wear today, or on the car visor or mirror or gas tank cap

- on the next few sheets of toilet tissue or Kleenex
- on a beautiful cake or outrageously large cookie (mini-messages needed here)
- on a note pinned to his pj's
- on a fake prescription. Example: Rx for a lonely lady (me): an evening dancing cheek to cheek with you. When?
- on a huge pizza, using the veggies of your choice.
- on a poster set on an easel and displayed in the living room so he can see it when he comes in
- in a letter, tucked into his sock or underwear drawer

❀ ❀ ❀

On February 14 or any day, hand him your lovingest valentine canister full of candy hearts with sentimental messages of love.

❀ ❀ ❀

Rent space in the personal column of the newspaper. To keep intruders out of your private business, use nicknames or initials. Highlight your wonderful words with a fluorescent pen and leave the paper around where he will be sure to see it. Example:

- Mr. Magic — How about Saturday night at seven?
- We've got it all!
- Let's make Sunday sizzle. I've got ideas.
- You really are the sunshine of my life.
- I still do! I still do!

❀ ❀ ❀

Purchase a car bumper sticker that says, "I love my husband [wife]."

❀ ❀ ❀

Add a touch of romance by writing your note on pretty parchment paper, then roll it in a scroll and tie it with a slim black or scarlet ribbon.

❀ ❀ ❀

Write a happiness report:

- "The best part of Sunday afternoon was when you flopped down on the bed beside me for a long talk while we lay in each other's arms. I felt very close to you then."

- "The closer I get to our house each evening, the heavier my foot gets on the accelerator on the way home from work. I can't wait to see you and tell you things that happened."
- "I feel close to you when we are learning new things together, like ballroom dancing, or when we took the course about investing in stocks and bonds. When we visit new churches or leave a dance or theater or cross a busy street holding hands, I feel like somebody's girlfriend."

❀ ❀ ❀

Send a copy of an old love letter, maybe one you wrote while dating. Let him know you still feel the same.

❀ ❀ ❀

Mail a loving note to your spouse at work. Mark it personal or confidential. Make it as intimate or heartfelt as you like:

- "Just to let you know you are on my mind today."

- "Surprises when you get home tonight. See you then!"
- "I'm showering at eight. Join me?"
- "You mean everything to me."

❀ ❀ ❀

Thinking that the personal message you cooked up may be a little too hot to handle if his secretary happens to intercept? Then send it in code. Tell him to look in his coat pocket for the secret decoder. You remember the code, don't you? . . . the one you used as a kid: A=1, B=2, C=3, etc.

□ From Jo: "I use finger paints to write what I want to say on my front or back or chest or breast or any other part of my anatomy. If he doesn't find it, I give clues to help. Sure gets his full attention!"

❀ ❀ ❀

Bring out the grins by signing off with your kissiest red lipstick imprint so he will know your letter is authentic.

❀ ❀ ❀

Spray your love letter with cologne, or enclose a little satin pillow of fragrance or two packets of bubble bath. Little samples of perfume tucked in magazine ads are perfect to enclose, too.

❀ ❀ ❀

Send your love a telegram. Imagine how surprised he'll be when the Western Union operator reads it to him on the phone. Will she blush? Will he? Wonderful fun! Here are a couple of ideas for classical thinkers:

> *As boundless as the sea,*
> *My love as deep;*
> *The more I give thee,*
> *The more I have,*
> *For both are infinite.*
> JULIET, IN SHAKESPEARE'S
> *ROMEO AND JULIET*

> *(On his birthday)*
> *Grow old along with me. The best is yet*
>   *to be.*
> RABBI BEN EZRA

> *But thou dost make the very night itself*
>   *brighter than day.*
> H. W. LONGFELLOW

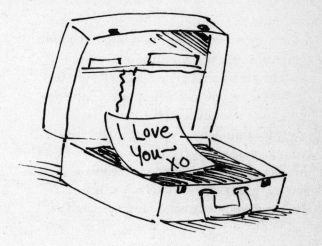

*Make your sweetie's heart skip a beat by leaving
your written expression of love in a book he is
reading or stick your letter in his briefcase or
leave it on his pillow sometime when you will be
away for the night.*

❀ ❀ ❀

Write down your original wedding vows.
If you penned them yourself, all the better.
Sign them in your own handwriting and
add a love phrase like "I still feel the same
today."

❀ ❀ ❀

Not too good at writing? Greeting cards are a
graphic way of underscoring your love. There
are literally thousands that tell it like you feel
it. Whenever you locate the perfect one every
now and then, buy it on the spot to be put
away for future use. Send one a day when
your love is flowing freely or forty because it's
his fortieth birthday or one a week for a
month "just because." Too busy to shop?
Peruse mail-order catalogs from places like:

Leanin' Tree
Box 9800
Boulder, CO 80301

The Scriptorium (Inspirational)
P.O. Box 3127
Catonsville, MD 21228-0127

Born to Be Cherished

To love and be loved is the greatest joy on earth

*Romance cannot be put into quantity
production — the moment love becomes casual,
it becomes commonplace.*

FREDERICK LEWIS ALLEN, *Only Yesterday*

Howard J. Markman, director of the University of Denver's Center for Marital and Family Studies, notes that divorce can be accurately predicted with 90 percent accuracy using these factors as indicators: The amount of invalidation, criticism, and put-downs exchanged between partners, as well as the measure of indifference shown.

"In the last analysis, love is only the reflection of a person's own worthiness from other persons," said Ralph Waldo Emerson. People crave appreciation and approval. Somehow, all of us are dependent on the affirmation of those near and dear to us to replenish a sense of dignity that God planned for us and to rid ourselves of spells of discouragement and pessimism. A pat on the back is instant therapy.

An author friend of mine says, "When my husband cheers me on, I suddenly develop a new burst of power to write — better, faster, and longer." One woman I know called her husband at his office, saying, "This is the president of the John Johnson Fan Club. I just called to say 'I love you.'" Such random acts of enthusiastic encouragement build self-esteem, reduce friction, and oil the wheels of any relationship. Are you your spouse's biggest fan?

Here are ideas from women who have learned to fine-tune small basic routines so they are magically transformed into positives:

❀ ❀ ❀

My husband is a carpenter. I run my own computer business from a plushy office. We both work hard, but I get paid more. He wears jeans and plaid flannel shirts and comes home with dirty hands. I often wear silk blouses and high heels. When my business cards were made up, I thought he felt cheated. Sometimes, more status is given to white-collar workers or those who work in nice places. So, on Father's Day, our two teenagers and I had his very own oversized "Best Father, Best Carpenter, Best Husband, Best Looking" cards made up. He proudly handed them out to fellow employees and subcontractors the following week.

❀ ❀ ❀

Compliment your good guy specifically once every day this week about personal habits or character traits or favors done. Maybe this is the right time to pat him on the back for vacuuming your car, repairing your sewing box, or phoning your mother every day when you were sick. Have you told him lately that he is a good provider? A great lover? That he has a great sense of humor? That you like to see him in the yard playing ball with the kids?

Here is what to say to let him know you appreciate all those terrific values that keep your relationship thriving, but that no one ever mentions much:

- One of the things I appreciate most about you is _____
_____.
- You make me feel loved when _____
_____.
- I like the way you handled things when _____.
- I admire you because _____
_____
(you seldom use foul language, are dependable, honest, clean, think things through when it comes to religious ideas, etc.).
- I feel loved and safe with you.
- Everybody should be married to someone like you.
- You have always made a good living for us. Thanks for working so hard.
- I thought about us several times today. I'm satisfied.

❀ ❀ ❀

Fill a bowl with written thank-yous, then ask your spouse to draw one out each day until the bowl is empty.

❀ ❀ ❀

If you keep a journal, read a passage aloud that tells how much you love him.

❀ ❀ ❀

Pray privately for your spouse. When you feel close after loving or when you wake up next to him in the night or when you catch a glimpse of him peacefully going about difficult or mundane chores like shoveling snow or mowing grass, just freeze a moment and silently ask God's blessing. Remind the Lord of your partner's needs and wants and hopes. If you don't, who will? Tell him about your praying.

❀ ❀ ❀

Sit down beside him for no special reason. Watch the hummingbirds. Sit close in the twilight on the back-porch glider and listen to the crickets or pet the cat on your lap. Rest your head on his shoulder or slip an arm around him. Shared peacefulness with no pressure leaves freedom for enjoying and appreciating each other and opens the door to good talk or the pleasure of silence. He will know how much having him near means when you ignore the phone.

19

❀ ❀ ❀

Touch! Stroke! Hug! Hold hands or link fingers while walking in the mall. Snuggle and cuddle. Try all kinds of hugs and name each one: bear hugs, back-to-back, tummy-touching hugs, bun bangers, wraparounds, back-to-front. Hold him close for no reason, yes, right there in the kitchen, for as long as it feels good to both of you. Tell him how much you love falling asleep in his arms.

❀ ❀ ❀

Write an "I Need You Because" letter. Be specific.

- I need you as a companion because
  _____.

- I need you as a husband/provider because _____.
- I need you as a lover because _____.
- I need you as a friend to share my spiritual side because _____.
- I need you as a father to our children because _____.

❀ ❀ ❀

Propose a toast to your spouse at a quiet birthday dinner for two, telling his best traits aloud. Do you admire him because he is bright, flirty, fun, tough, eccentric? What?

Bonus idea #1: Plan ahead, then invite best pals to tell their positive thought about your OK guy on videotape. The two of you can "hunker down" under the afghan in front of the television set for a surprise showing after his birthday cake is cut. He will get the feeling that he is "all kinds of wonderful," just as you hoped.

Bonus idea #2: Ask each dinner guest to bring along a twenty-word toast for your grown-up birthday boy; then after dessert, everybody will read theirs aloud.

❀ ❀ ❀

When he fixes things or has been nice enough to do something special like straightening up your overdrawn checking account, leave little sunburst notes here and there:

- (On the refrigerator): Thanks for fixing_____
  for me _____
  when I was having too-hot flashes about the kids bringing home that

stray cat. You cooled me down nicely just when I needed it.
- (On the car steering wheel): Glad you aligned the tires on the car. I was getting a bum steer.
- (On the lawn mower): I appreciate your three hours of backbreaking yard bravery clearing away the thorns and thistles beside the hedge. It looks *so* much better now.

❀ ❀ ❀

Purchase a blank awards certificate at an office supply store for your wonderful "white knight." If you like, buy a kit and learn calligraphy to fancy it all up. Put something on it like:

Good Deed Award to My Mate

You have my "Good Housekeeping Seal of Approval" for:

- Valor in taking care of me when I broke my leg.
- Courage to hug me and the kids even when we all had colds and you didn't.
- Patience without complaining

when my brother overstayed his
welcome.
- Ingenuity for outstanding
bedroom performance last
night.
- Good homekeeping all last
month when my sick mom
needed me in Cincinnati.

❀ ❀ ❀

So your Mr. Ordinary never won a blue
ribbon? Here's your chance to turn the
mundane into something memorable. All
you do is buy something at a trophy store
and bestow the "Front-Runner Award" of
the year. He can be the world's best of anything—left-handed tennis or guitar player,
handyman, or dance partner.

❀ ❀ ❀

Bang the drums of affirmation by stringing
a banner across the front entrance that says:

- "Home of the World's Greatest Little
  League Coach!"
- "A Great Golfer Lives Here!"
- "We Knew You Could Do It!"
- "Welcome Home, Joe!"

✽ ✽ ✽

Scrawl your message with chalk on the front sidewalk or driveway or share the fun with neighbors by chalking up the blacktop on your cul-de-sac.

✽ ✽ ✽

Long-term commitment: When laying new cement for a cellar floor, patio, pool, driveway, or sidewalk, suggest that the two of you stand side by side to make permanent "his and hers" footprints in the wet cement.

✽ ✽ ✽

Your spouse can say hello to a few "positive perceptions" about himself if you name things after him. Your vacation home could be Spencer's Spot; your boat *The Mr. J.;* your beloved and very expensive English bulldog who has become a member of your family might be Little John. One woman says she entered a contest with a prize-winning recipe named after her husband: Marvelous Marvin's Marvelous Muffins.

✽ ✽ ✽

If you have been pleased as punch to be Mrs. John Jacobovich for seventeen years, say so! Tell him how proud you are that he chose you out of all the rest to share that name with him. One good name deserved another when the two of you got hitched, right?

❋ ❋ ❋

Stowing away cards and notes sent by your true love will let him know how much you appreciate his thoughtfulness. Stick them in the family Bible, a shoe box, or a scrapbook to be read together some time in the future. Give back an especially meaningful one as your gift to him every now and then. Let him know that you are doing it because you loved the message.

❋ ❋ ❋

Make up your own little love book. Whenever you think of another reason he is a standout guy, just jot it down, one per page: "Alice loves Norman because . . ." After a while you'll have a complete book of compliments, and won't he love that? Deliver it in a heart-shaped box wherever he will be on Valentine's Day or his birthday. If he travels a lot on business, arrange with the flight attendant that he receive it as a surprise during the flight. He'll have plenty of time to appreciate your sentimental sayings.

❀ ❀ ❀

Play up a pet nickname for your partner. If he's your Bugsy Bunny, buy a bunny stamp and stamp pad for decorating mundane things like grocery lists. Maybe he's more like a cuddly teddy bear; find bear mugs, greeting cards, coin banks. Or specialize in teddy lingerie.

❀ ❀ ❀

Keep a Look Book (that's a photo album), and write appreciative remarks beside some of the pictures that are most likely to get special attention as he thumbs through:

- Look at Ken's perfect diving form!
- Bald is beautiful and sexy on Ken and Telly Sevalas.
- Ken is forty! Aged to perfection.
- Ken, taking me to the doctor for the twenty-first time in 1989 before Jennifer was born. Outstanding performance, Ken!

❀ ❀ ❀

Put the man in your life on display by stra-
tegically placing his photo atop your desk
at work for others to see. Tell him what
you did. He'll feel good knowing you think
of him during the day. If he visits, he can
see for himself how proud you are of the
one you married.

❀ ❀ ❀

Type all of your compliments and affirma-
tions on a brand-new Rolodex file, or write
them on individual file cards to be stored
in a terrific-looking file box painted his
favorite color or stenciled with his name.
It's all for his desk, of course. Ask him to
read one every day as long as they last and
an extra whenever he feels blue or discouraged.

❀ ❀ ❀

He'll see how much you value him if you keep
a special place for mementos of your shared
lives, maybe in a fancy box, scrapbook, or
drawer. Here's where you stow away precious
photos, clippings, awards, certificates, and
other things you cherish.

❀ ❀ ❀

Feeling your feelings won't hurt you! For
no reason at all, look at him directly and
keep the gaze, then tell him how much you
love him. Such acts won't come easily for
people who have kept their deepest thoughts
under cover for years. You might become
misty-eyed, but tell him why you think he is
terrific, anyway. Give five reasons. Let him
know that you need him and why.

❀ ❀ ❀

Affirm his roots, his beginnings, his traditions, even if they are very different from
yours. Speak as well of his family as you
can. Compile a family cookbook by calling
uncles, aunts, and cousins for his favorite
recipes. Using your computer will make it
easy. If he is Polish or German, learn to
dance the polka just like his parents did.
Make up a batch of fettucine every month
and freeze it just because his Italian mother
always had extra on hand. Hang the calories! You've got a marriage to tend!

❀ ❀ ❀

Perhaps you awakened from your Cinderella
dream long ago, but you can still affirm

each other by restating your wedding vows at ten years, twenty-five, or even fifty. It's a very meaningful way to celebrate an anniversary and show how much you value your relationship. Your pastor may have ideas for a short ceremony, or you could just read the vows together from the Book of Common Prayer, holding hands in the quiet of your own living room. Some cruise lines regularly offer a renewal of vows with the chaplain as part of a seven-day vacation package. Ask your travel agent.

❀ ❀ ❀

As often as you can, when you get up in the morning, be as friendly to your spouse as you would be to house guests. As he sleepily trundles off to the bathroom for a morning shower, wouldn't it be nice to ask, "Did you sleep OK last night, Hon?" or "How are you feeling today?" or to say, "It will be a good day today," or "I'm glad you're here to drink coffee with me." Simple pleasantness and positiveness can generate many good feelings.

❀ ❀ ❀

You'll never lose by respecting your partner's uniqueness, his idiosyncrasies, and his passionate preferences. Does he love white shirts? books by Tom Clancy? lots of space and privacy? quotes from Ephesians? keyboard by Yanni? golf magazines? Chinese food? If he is crazy about highlighter pens to mark up favorite books, sneak a new supply into the desk drawer when he isn't looking. Is he interested in stamps? Then bring home the newest releases next time you visit the post office. One woman whose husband loves gardening wrote to an aged relative for an envelope of "those ancient muskmelon seeds that no one can find in stores anymore." Maybe your spouse is nuts about nougat or chocolate from Switzerland. Hiding a whole box or just a few in a lunch bag will bring a knowing grin at noon. Catering to his wish list and getting it right when you buy gifts or stock the pantry or bring books or videos from the library lets him know you appreciate him, just as he is.

❀ ❀ ❀

When you go through magazines or newspapers, highlight news about famous folks sharing his family name.

❀ ❀ ❀

Clip or mark interesting things in the newspaper so he won't miss them.

❀ ❀ ❀

Serve pizza on Friday nights or fried green tomatoes just because he loves them.

❀ ❀ ❀

Buy whipped butter because he believes it contains fewer calories.

❀ ❀ ❀

Opposites attract. Have you told him that you love him anyway when he takes a day of your vacation to go sloshwicking (yes, there is such a thing) or to attend the Glockenspielers' Convention?

❀ ❀ ❀

If he doesn't attend church with you right now, just accept it without comment. Recall often that we are not responsible for the other's faith, only our own.

Love is very patient and kind.
1 CORINTHIANS 13:4, TLB

31

❀ ❀ ❀

When he shares feelings of sadness or dis-
appointment or grief or anger, validate
your partner by just listening, without criticism. Everyone has a right to feel as they
do. Have you tried using the words, "I understand"? Dr. C. Menninger notes, "Love
cures people, both the ones who give it and
the ones who receive it." You could help
by saying:

- "I wish I could hug away the hurt for
  you."
- "How can I help?"
- "What one thing would make you feel
  better?"
- "How shall I pray for you?"

❀ ❀ ❀

Get a passion for whatever his is. Poke
your head in his workshop or studio or
hobby room every now and then to ask,
"What are you working on now?" or to
say, "Those bookends you made would
probably bring seventy-five dollars at a
craft sale." Bring home items to add to his
collection of baseball caps or classical
CDs or orchid plants. Maybe you can get

his favorite author to autograph a copy of her new book when she signs at the local bookstore. When you travel together, you can help search out clown or cat prints because your partner loves them, or World War II relics or Jean Harlow posters. Does he have the hots for hot peppers? You'll get a big bang for your buck spent on a salsa cookbook at a neighborhood garage sale.

❀ ❀ ❀

It's your move to become an encourager when your mate's emotional tank seems empty. Maybe he feels like he's running on fumes working overtime starting a new business on a shoestring, or is faced with subpoenas and difficult hearings in a court trial, or is without a job. Is he having trouble losing weight despite what the doctor said? Is he performing a solo for the first time with the community chorus? How about a Siskel and Ebert "thumbs-up" at appropriate times, like when he heads out the door? Or, could you blow a kiss? He will think, "She cares enough to stick with me no matter what."

❀ ❀ ❀

Encouraging things to say:

- "I think you are getting better at ___ ."
- "Things are seldom as bad as they seem."
- "Joy cometh in the morning."
- "The best is yet to come."
- "I appreciate you when _____ ."
- "Your great personality and long-time computer experience are going to carry you a long way when you apply for jobs."
- "I'll be thinking about you today when you interview for that job you want so much."
- "Making up new recipes is where you shine. You could write a cookbook."
- "I am proud of you when _____ ."

If you love someone . . . you will always believe in him, always expect the best of him, and always stand your ground in defending him.

1 CORINTHIANS 13:7, TLB

◻ They all said he was a crackpot. Nobody thought that he would amount to anything; nobody, that is, except his wife. Everybody laughed at all the hours he spent tinkering in his workshop. Often, when he got home from working ten hours a day for about eleven dollars a week at the local electric company, he would be engrossed in making up his ideas into concrete objects until the wee hours of the morning. His wife was so sure his engine would work that she held the oil lamp night after night for three years so he could put his crazy contraption together with wires, nuts, and bolts, often in freezing cold weather. Henry Ford was just thirty years old when the first horseless carriage lurched out of his garage, much to the astonishment of neighbors. Guess who was riding beside him in the front seat?

❀ ❀ ❀

Has life given you and your partner rough treatment lately? Let others schedule expensive trips to the land of martinis and bikinis to unload tension. Ingenious folks like you can come up with better ideas. Print out a poster offering your stressed-out guy a silly or serious Saturday and Sunday smorgasbord of fun and relaxing things to do with you. Maybe you'll find just what you're looking for in the weekend creative loafing section of the local newspaper, or work up a list of your own ideas. Have him place an *X* by his favorites, then go for one or two. It's amazing what is available right under your nose when you bother to check things out. We found:

- The Bald Is Beautiful Convention in North Carolina. (Their philosophy is, "We believe that skin is in. We don't have room for drugs, plugs, or rugs.")
- The Onion Harvester Hoedown; see Miss Onion crowned.
- The Watermelon Festival. There's a watermelon-seed-spitting contest and a Kiss-the-Pig Contest, with a prize for the Best Porker Pucker.
- The World Catfish Festival at Belzoni, Mississippi.

❀ ❀ ❀

Other ideas:

- A day of hugging, kissing, talking, loving, listening to Otis Redding CDs, especially "Sitting on the Dock of the Bay," because it reminds you of your honeymoon in Hawaii.

- Spend time reading aloud from *Couples in Love*, a day-by-day turnover calendar of 366 quotes on love and marriage (Garborg's, Bloomington, Minn.).
- A retreat day when you will read inspirational things to each other, listen to inspiring songs, pray at length about matters important to both of you right now, or plan for your future. (Maybe your church's pastor will have suggestions.)
- Drive around looking for a new house to buy.
- Do the spring housecleaning together.
- Go to the outlet mall.
- Plan a minidate at McDonald's for all the hamburgers and French fries you can eat.
- Spend a day at the carnival riding the loop-de-loop and eating cotton candy, hot dogs, and other lovely forbidden grub.

• See chapter 8 for hundreds of other
fun—yet inexpensive—things to do.

❀ ❀ ❀

When your partner fails at something or is
feeling especially disappointed, remind him
that "Your worth is not in what you do,
but in who you are." Read together
Romans 8 and Ephesians 3:17-21 from the
Bible.

❀ ❀ ❀

Someone has said that love is the only passion which includes in its dreams the happiness of someone else. Write down a few
of the wishes and goals your partner has
shared in casual conversation from time
to time. Does he wish he had money to
own an expensive Old English sheepdog
(even if you don't), or buy Aquatred tires
for his car or get it painted, even if it is
seven years old? To take a course in German? Take a trip to visit distant relatives
in Europe? Go camping with you? Surprise him by getting out your list every
once in a while. Tell him you want to talk
about how the two of you can make at
least one of those dreams come true in the

next few weeks or months or years and how you can finance and carry out a plan. It's like saying, "Your hopes and aspirations count, too."

❀ ❀ ❀

When did you get to be grown-ups? When you signed for your first mortgage? When your first child was born? Nonsense. It was when you learned to balance life's heavy responsibilities against the "kid" inside each of you. So, today you will lighten up. Push the kids' schoolbooks and jackets off the pool table in the garage and get going on a fast-paced tournament. Dig out the baseball gloves for a great game of catch. Head out for the swimming pool at the park and be there the minute it opens to play a game of Keep Away before the crowd arrives. Race each other. Throw the ball over the roof for a game of Andy Andy Over just like you did growing up. Enjoying the other is just another way of saying, "I love having you around."

❀ ❀ ❀

Get silly together. Experts say that laughter connects and heals relationships and illnesses, too. Gentle teasing or tickling or cracking up over outrageous jokes and crazy puns or silly sentences takes the stress out of life and promotes good feelings toward each other.

❀ ❀ ❀

Laugh at his jokes in front of company, even though you've heard them all before.

❀ ❀ ❀

It's OK for him to overhear you praying for him or thanking God for bringing him into your life.

❀ ❀ ❀

Quiet folks need special attention. Introduce him proudly and with a smile to other guests at a party. Don't let him become invisible. Break the ice with lots of get-acquainted information, and lead him into good conversation with others so he doesn't feel left out or get the feeling you've forgotten him.

❀ ❀ ❀

If once in a while he gets deeply moved to tears in front of others, take over the conversation for him. Most men feel that crying is a sign of weakness, even though we women know better and call it tenderness. He'll know you understand his feelings.

❊ ❊ ❊

One family counselor notes, "Couples often do not realize how much they stand in the way of the other's enjoyment of individual interests." There is great value in keeping some things separate. Encourage him to have a few good friends and activities on his own. What greater gift than allowing each other the personal freedom of time apart spent playing cards with buddies, taking ski lessons, or participating in a local theater group without guilt? His weekend of reminiscing with old college friends would probably not be enhanced by your presence, either. In such matters, an understanding spouse can generate happy ripples in a relationship. Encouraging him to enjoy such separate events relays the message, "I trust you; I appreciate the differences in us, and I want you to be happy," and affirms his ability to handle everything responsibly.

❀ ❀ ❀

Affirmation and forgiveness are civilized traits, especially when they come forth at unexpected times:

- From Karen Burton Mains: "How terrible to be the unloved one. I've known times when I didn't feel like loving my husband. But in the middle of horrifying emptiness, I discovered that love is renewable. It's strictly a matter of choice. Countless times, I've chosen to love when I thought I had every reason not to respond or care. I've often dropped to my knees, asking the God of love to fill me with enough for my most human husband. When I relinquished my rights in prayer, when I forgave my husband for his inconsideration or misunderstanding, when I focused on his positive qualities, when I asked the Lord for special power, then I could love again.

  "When I bring a bit of God into my husband's life like this, I am elevated from my position of family car controller, storekeeper, detailing computer, vacuum pusher, and laundry sorter. I am something holy."

*Spend a day at the carnival riding the
loop-de-loop and eating cotton candy, hot dogs,
and other lovely forbidden grub.*

Getting Sentimental
over You

How to become an old softie and enjoy it

If you would be loved, love and be lovable.

BENJAMIN FRANKLIN, *Poor Richard*

Let's hear it for romance! And slushy sentiment!

OK, you may roll your eyes. Two hearts
aglow after all the years you two have
been together? Yes, indeed! And let's not
rule out men when it comes to softhearted
notions.

Everyone has sentimental ideas of their
own. Your personal day in, day out love
scenes may not live up to courtship fantasies. They may fall short of the romantic
raptures described by the world's poets and
fiction writers, but even in this new age of

garishly graphic cinema and sleazy magazine articles, tenderness is definitely not outmoded. Two soft hearts beating as one is a necessity in a well-tended relationship.

One well-known counselor whose special interest is problems that affect high-powered working couples holds firmly to the theory that the way to preserve a marriage and keep the rough edges smooth is to devote a certain amount of time to romance. She contends that heartfelt sentiment is the emotional dynamic that prevents couples from becoming unfeeling robots.

Little sentimental things connect people. Some of the expressions of love suggested here reflect Victorian romance, while others match today's styles. They are designed to set free the wonderfully complicated and sometimes secret sweetheart feelings we harbor but are afraid to express to those nearest and dearest to us.

❀ ❀ ❀

Carry your partner's photo in your wallet to go everywhere you do. Or have a snapshot taken of the two of you just for that purpose. Admire it appropriately when he is around, and take a good long look when the two of you are out among other people.

❀ ❀ ❀

Have your wedding certificate triple-matted, then fitted into the most expensive gold or mahogany fashion frame you can find (thrift shops often have these at affordable marked-down prices). Hang it conspicuously. Tell him how proud you are to be married to him. Later, dig out one of your wedding invitations to place beside it. After that, enlarge the display to include your wedding portrait and photos taken when you were dating. Have fun recalling details.

❀ ❀ ❀

Everybody knows that life has its ups and downs. Assemble photos of your best and worst times together in an album to give as a surprise anniversary gift. People who have toughed it out together have something good going for them, and they know it.

❀ ❀ ❀

Do you yearn to bring the sentimental things you see in movies into your own life? Then tell him you would love to walk in the rain holding hands or kiss on the beach as the sun is setting or do the anniversary waltz in front of your children while celebrating your silver wedding anniversary. Maybe he will reveal untold daydreams, too, if you risk telling yours first.

❀ ❀ ❀

Make a marriage memory display. Buy a bulletin board and tack on meaningful old photos, precious postcards, ticket stubs from wonderful concerts and plays, newspaper clippings, long-forgotten restaurant menus, dried bouquets, special letters sent back and forth, announcements of job promotions or baby births, and other things you cherish. Perhaps your mate has a sentimental greeting card or note hidden away to be added to the memorabilia. You'll feel closer as you reminisce about everything, because you and your partner are the only ones who shared the intimacies and know the whole story.

❀ ❀ ❀

Had a wonderfully intimate vacation in Hawaii? Recreate it in your own living room with the appropriate music, grass skirt, a flower in your hair, a meal of sushi and pineapple, and a video about Waikiki. Then invite your mate to get his rear into low gear as you swing and sway to the hula just like you did back then. Only you two can relive the sentimental details tonight.

❀ ❀ ❀

Hang a good times dateline map, mark a happy event for each date, then dare to relive and reminisce about those best events. So once you rented a room at Hotel Hotstuff for a sensational sneak get-away? Is it noted on your dateline? Did you run off to Las Vegas for a winning weekend? Did love become new once again the night you moved into your first home? Did you giggle for days about hiding in the basement from an inconvenient knock on the door by an obnoxious neighbor? Only the two of you can share the whole romantic or sentimental or silly scoop behind each event.

❀ ❀ ❀

Linda mailed wedding photos to her "Best Bubba's" office on their fifteenth anniversary. Hank told her later that he shut the door and spent the noon hour reminiscing.

❀ ❀ ❀

When he asks what you want for your anniversary or birthday gift, ask him to please have a big photo taken of himself, just because you get lonesome for him at work sometimes. That's the one you will hang on your office wall.

❀ ❀ ❀

Buy a fancy double picture frame that folds. Have a brand-new glamour shot taken of yourself in your best duds for one side. Of course, his photo goes in the other. Display it prominently so he can be delighted coming in the door from work. Bet he would enjoy a little hand-printed card that says, "You've made my life complete."

❀ ❀ ❀

Have a favorite old-time photo showing his mother and father and him as a baby blown up to poster size to be framed and hung on your family portrait wall. Point out to guests what a beautiful baby he was and that your handsome child looks just like him.

❀ ❀ ❀

Have an aerial photograph taken of the first home you bought where you raised your kids for ten years, or his grandparents' farm where he was brought up, or his hometown, or any other sentimental place. Have it blown up, framed, and on full display on your living-room or dining-room wall. Be sure to type up pertinent information on a permanent label to attach to the back so your grandchildren will know the whole story.

❑ From Mert: "We got out my pregnancy journal, now ten years old, to read together. In *The Daily Me*, every morning I had written down things like how I felt blessed to have this baby growing inside me and my hopes and plans for us and the child that would be growing up in our home. I wrote of the new closeness I felt when the two of us listened together to the baby's heartbeat or watched my belly move when she kicked. He said he never knew before."

❀ ❀ ❀

Remember those early days when you
couldn't think of anything but each
other? Recall what it was that attracted
you to him in the beginning, then tell him.
Green eyes? A flashing smile? A solid,
straight chin? His caring attitude? Now
it is years later. Pondering these things
often and letting him know will keep your
love strong.

❀ ❀ ❀

Recycle exquisite moments by actually
returning to sentimental places. Go back to
the spot where he proposed. Do something
you did before. Wear the same outfit or a
similar one. Dare to say the same things to
each other. Ask him to slip the engagement
ring on once again. Take a deep breath and
kiss with a promise. Marvel at the miracle
of how you met and how you ended up
together in spite of all you went through
while dating.

❀ ❀ ❀

Tape a Just Married sign to the back of
your car; then return for a night to the
same room of your honeymoon hotel for a

repeat performance. Can he carry his best girl over the threshold? Relive the romance.

❋ ❋ ❋

Take a sentimental journey back in time by getting out that box of mementos saved since dating days. Plan an evening to read the tender notes scrawled on old restaurant menus that you saved, reminisce over concert and movie ticket stubs, imprinted match books, vacation brochures, hotel and park admission receipts. Cherish the special times brought to mind by trinkets bought in gift shops at faraway places. Read love letters aloud to him, and choose one for him to read to you. Overcome your shyness and swing and sway in the living room to your special song. Haven't got a personal memory box? Then start one and begin making plans to use it in years ahead. You'll be glad you did.

❋ ❋ ❋

Plan a spring travel spree back to where it all began. Revisit a couple of towns where you once lived, maybe before the two of you got together. Everything will be different; maybe downtown will have moved to the neighborhood mall. But perhaps the old homestead is still there. How fascinating to know that some new owner added a front porch or painted it blue or ugly pink! You will want to point out which upstairs window in your parents' former home was your bedroom. Recall aloud how you and your best friend hooted and whistled at that cute boy who lived across the street. Mom predicted he never would make much of himself, but of course, he later became a famous psychiatrist. Or take a sentimental journey back to an alma mater to see if they tore down your dorm or whether your team's trophy is still on display.

❀ ❀ ❀

Better than TV! Get out high school yearbooks for an evening of laughs. How about that hairdo? Can you find your faces in the chorus lineup? Tell him all about those growing-up years, the Elvis and *Casablanca* posters in your bedroom, your secret love who was later arrested for stealing cars (or did he become a big-time wealthy Texas oilman?), or the time you were locked out after a midnight date.

Turn to photos of you in the drama club, then recall how you dreamed of becoming a Hollywood actress.

❀ ❀ ❀

Right after Valentine's Day, buy up sentimental cards at close-out prices. Send these loving "darts to his heart" via U.S. mail all year. At least once, include a tender and meaningful memento like a lock of your hair.

❀ ❀ ❀

On their anniversary, one wife covered her husband's desk with heart-shaped balloons and red paper hearts cut from construction paper. Of course, she scribbled mushy messages on each.

❀ ❀ ❀

Use two-sided adhesive tape to stick messages on the inside bottom of his desk or dresser drawer or on his workbench or drafting table. Use candy valentine hearts with words on them or sticky letters pulled from big alphabet sheets available at stationery stores. Leave short and sweetsy notes:

- The two of us make a forever team.
- My headache is gone.

- We've got it all!
- Thanks for your understanding.
- The luckiest day of my life was when I met you.
- The touch of your hand is the most wonderful feeling I can have.
- You are incredible!
- Each day I love you more.
- Thanks for the happiest twenty years of my life.
- You are mine forever.
- On Valentine's Day, hand your sweetie a canister full of these love messages. Leave a note for him to "take two each hour."

❀ ❀ ❀

It is probably legal to kidnap your man at work at about four-thirty in the afternoon and whisk him away to reenact your first date or the time he proposed in that fancy restaurant. Or perhaps it was at a roadside hideaway with the jukebox blaring? The two of you can do it all over again. Sit in the same booth. Maybe you can have wedding rings ready to exchange, the ones you never have been able to afford before. Have your favorite song played, and waltz or rock 'n' roll the night away for old times' sake. For added fun, invite the kids along to relive the memory with you. Just because you had to learn about being sentimental in marriage the hard way doesn't mean they have to, and they will be pleased that their mom and dad are still feeling so friendly toward each other.

□ From Ellen: "After everybody had left the silver wedding reception our children hosted for us, sentimental reminiscing set in. 'We have come a long way, maybe with not a lot of years left,' we told each other, remembering couples our age already separated by death. Then, each of us wrote down several things we wanted to do together in years ahead. Now, five years after, we have accomplished some, completing a financial management course, hiking part of the Appalachian Trail, learning to dry tomatoes (because he grows bushels), and organizing a family reunion. Without that time of sentimental dream sharing, we might never have gotten these pleasant things done. There are still many happy times to look forward to, and we plan to re-evaluate goals every few years."

❀ ❀ ❀

Use secret sign language and signals that have evoked sentiment over the years. During a party, delight each other with private endearments and intimate looks. Throw (or smack) a small kiss or give a "thumbs-up" when no one is looking. Glad-hand across the room. Tweak an ear because it has always meant you love him, or use sign language or foreign phrases or mumbo jumbo that only the two of you know. Make inside jokes in front of strangers.

❀ ❀ ❀

Were you traveling by train or air on a special day like your anniversary or birthday or when he told you he was dropping best girlfriend Margie Smith for you? Now you're taking a trip again. Take along a ready-to-go package of surprises to stir up today's sentiments. Bet a well-paid waiter or flight attendant could be persuaded to deliver a small floral bouquet and something for a toast to celebrate these reminiscences in style. All you have to add are hugs and kisses and some old-fashioned words straight from your heart: "To Tom: I'd elope with you all over again."

> ❑ One of the most precious things I own is a copy of the palm print of my husband's hand made on my Xerox machine. It clearly shows all the little lines and marks that I know so well and, best of all, the wedding ring I placed on his third finger years ago that he never removes. It is such an intimate likeness, even better than a photograph because it is so incredibly unique, so personal and familiar.

❀ ❀ ❀

Prepare six sentimental celebrations this year to keep the love flowing and let him know you care. Make excuses to hold a party for two. Buy a half-dozen little bags of confetti, twelve blow-out party toys, and twelve party hats. For example:

- January 10—the day we met
- March 1—the day you were born. I'm so grateful!

- May 3—a memorable midnight date on the back-porch glider

❀ ❀ ❀

Keep a mistletoe sprig hanging around for an excuse to get passionate-on-the-spot all year. Move it from time to time so it appears as a surprise over his shower or closet or garage door, and be on the scene at the appropriate moment. Better yet, carry a mistletoe tidbit with you all day on Valentine's Day or on his birthday to hang hurriedly at promising places.

❀ ❀ ❀

Does he need extra kisses to know how much he is cherished? Pack exactly 100 foil-covered chocolate or twist-wrapped saltwater taffy kisses in a heart-shaped box that you have decorated especially for him. Tell him to take two as needed fifty times this year and that you'd like to share the real thing with him each time. Reminisce about your first kiss.

Bonus idea: Anything but ordinary will get his attention. Have a red ink stamp-pad kit made up so you can stamp luscious lip prints hither and yon when you want him to know how you feel about him. Great idea for jazzing up plain gift-wrapping paper, too.

❀ ❀ ❀

Take a picnic and a stroll to watch the sunset and carve your initials on a log or maybe write your names in the dirt on the ground with a stick. When the full moon comes up (take a look at your calendar to plan this perfectly!), walk back to the car hand in hand in the moonlight. Whisper sweet things even if you haven't done that for a very long time, and even if it feels a little uncomfortable. If all goes as planned, you'll remember this for a long, long time. So will he.

❀ ❀ ❀

Park at a favorite spot beside the lake, just like old times. Good behavior doesn't count tonight!

❑ From Allie: "I know how difficult it is for my husband to let go and cry when he is sad. When his beloved hunting dog died and I guessed that there were sentimental tears shed in private, I wrote a note in calligraphy

that simply said, 'I'm sorry. I loved
Fetch, too.' He told me later that it
meant a lot because nobody else
seemed to realize how much he cared
about his longtime buddy. The note
was kept in his desk drawer for a
long time."

❧ ❧ ❧

Become noteworthy. Write sentimental
notes or copy love poems on Post-it notes
and leave them everywhere. Tape one to
the sandwich in his briefcase, on the coffeepot or cup, inside his medicine cabinet or
sock drawer, to the shirt he will wear
today, on the car visor or mirror or gas
tank cap, on his pillow, the morning paper,
his aftershave bottle, the television screen,
or stuff one in his jacket pocket. Maybe
he'll find them all today, maybe not, but
the leftovers will touch off a torrent of
inspiration later on.

Bonus idea: If you can get into his car
while it is parked in the workplace parking
lot, stick a sentimental greeting card under
the car visor or tape it to the steering
wheel.

❀ ❀ ❀

Save a sentimental greeting card he gave you, and set it up on the kitchen table for a week. Frame it later. Tell him how many times you have enjoyed reading it over and over.

❀ ❀ ❀

Whether he's a brawny bulldozer operator, a stouthearted marine, or a quiet book-keeper, he'll appreciate a heart-shaped cake to celebrate any special day like a wedding anniversary, his birthday, the day the two of you met, or his job promotion. How? Bake one nine-inch round cake and one nine-inch square cake. Remove cakes from tins. Cut the round cake in half. On a large baking sheet or platter, turn the square cake so that it's like a diamond, with one corner at the top. Place flat sides of the round cake next to the top two sides to form a heart. Dress it up with his favorite icing and decorate with colored roses (a rose of any color signifies love) and some sentimental words. Turn the lights low during dinner.

❀ ❀ ❀

Present him with a piece of friendship jewelry that matches yours — half of a gold heart, identical rings or neck chains or charms. The glint of gold will prompt pertinent questions from friends, and your answers will let them know you two enjoy belonging to each other. Tell him you like letting others know he is your partner.

❊ ❊ ❊

Remember when love songs put you both in perfect harmony? You can recapture the mood by bringing your song back to life:

- Send the words in an envelope to his place of work.
- Scrounge around to find the tape to be played when you are making love.
- Have the music playing on tape every evening for a week when he comes home from work.
- Ask a violinist (or anybody else from the band) to serenade the two of you at a candlelight restaurant dinner.
- Sing your song in the kitchen when you feel happy.

❊ ❊ ❊

Find a CD or tape with Mr. Right's name or love handle in the title or one that describes him to a tee. Tell him it reminds

*Tape a Just Married sign to the back of your car;
then return for a night to the same room
of your honeymoon hotel for a repeat
performance. Can he carry his best girl
over the threshold? Relive the romance.*

you of him or that you get sentimental over
him every time you hear it.

❀ ❀ ❀

One long-time wife says she has the local
radio station disc jockey play the couple's
favorite sentimental song each anniversary.
"We always look forward to listening
together during our dinner by candlelight,"
she notes.

> ❏ From Jean: "Every once in a while, I
> tape some romantic words that tell
> how I truly feel about my tough-as-
> nails guy. Then, on an ordinary day
> when he least suspects, I slip the cas-
> sette into the tape deck of his car,
> leave the switch on and the volume
> up. *Voila!* Instant inspiration and ado-
> ration on the way to work." Caution:
> Idea not practical on car-pool day.

❀ ❀ ❀

Rejoice in whatever sentimental intimacy
you have. When he is walking ahead, you
can pick him out of the crowd and think to
yourself, "I know that man inside and out
like nobody else in the world does." When

you are proud of him speaking in front of a group, only you, sitting a world away in the back row of the auditorium, know what a difficult time he had getting notes in order, or how hard the two of you worked to get his shirt collar just right, or how sad he is feeling inside because his mom is in a coma in the hospital, or that he chooses to refrain from shrimp hors d'oeuvres because they send his allergy into a wild spin. You are probably the only one who can gauge his confidence accurately by observing his posture as he walks across the stage. Though separated by a thousand people, these sentimental thoughts bring you close, very close. Tell him so.

A Gift Is Love
You Give Away
'Tis blessed to give creatively

Love is not getting, but giving; . . . it is goodness, and honor, and peace and pure living.

HENRY VAN DYKE, *Little Rivers: A Handful of Heather*

It's his birthday. Out from behind your back come three boxes of chocolate mint Girl Scout cookies (his favorite) that have been stowed away in the back of the freezer for three months, or a miniphoto of you and the kids sealed inside a paperweight for his desk. In January, the spring gardening catalog you knew he was itching to get his hands on is waiting in the mail pile when he gets home from work. Or, can you afford a garden tractor? Wow! No matter what the cost of your gift, if it is something that just fits, there is bound to be an exciting grand opening.

Maybe part of you wants to bring home the solid-gold ring he admired in the mall jewelry shop, but the wallet part of you doesn't. If you don't have much money and your mind isn't bulging with ideas, you could take a minicourse in low-cost, no-cost Gift Giving 101 by reading *Big Book of Great Gift Ideas* by Alice Chapin (Tyndale House, 1991). Some of the best-remembered presents will be little labors of love that fill a special need, like cleaning up his workshop because he hates to do it or keeping your promise to get yourself a checkup at the doctor. The main thing is to get it right. If he's dieting and you give five pounds of macadamia nuts or Hershey's chocolate—wrong! Keep an eye out for "just right" trinkets, cards, bookmarks, framed mottoes, and other gifts all year long and save money by hitting the sales. Not only will you be ready on special occasions, but your secret supply will be there to soothe ruffled tempers after an argument or to pamper him when he has the flu. One wife makes the first of every month his gift day "just because you are worth it."

Use the romance of ribbon and the grace of lace to turn attention away from price by matching your creativeness to his cravings and preferences. Make the wrapping unique and suited to him and the occasion. And don't forget to collect big and little boxes all year long in anticipation of celebrations ahead.

Timing is important, too. If he has been out of work for three months and your budget is busted (again), dig out those rolls of quarters and dimes that you forgot you had to buy him a job-hunting book. In summer, set out wildflowers and encouraging Scripture verses at his breakfast place every time there is a nerve-racking job interview. He will know you are thinking about him as he heads out the door.

Perhaps you can leave hints in obvious places to keep him guessing where you hid his birthday bounty. Your clues and cheers can send him charging through the house, searching jacket and sweater pockets, grappling to the bottom of the laundry hamper, or poking into cracks and crevices around the fireplace.

❀ ❀ ❀

Make up an acrostic using his name; then add
flattering words and phrases for each letter.
Enclose it with a note or use it as a banner.

❀ ❀ ❀

One wife asks, "Do you dare lay bare a whole
new concept of gift giving on your wedding
anniversary? Inexpensive bright blue paper
(or for those who dare, cellophane!), gift wrap
the girl in his life . . . you! Tie up this personal
package with a huge ribbon and attach a sign
that says 'Handle with Care.'"

❀ ❀ ❀

Ask his mother for that wonderful blue-
berry recipe he is always raving about and
bake up a cobbler, just for him.

❀ ❀ ❀

Buy a gallon of ice cream—pistachio, butterscotch, elderberry, or whatever is his
favorite. Wrap it pretty with two spoons
attached to the bow and feed each other.

❀ ❀ ❀

Are red raspberries his favorite? Today's
gift is a big basketful. You will offer to pre-

pare shortcake for supper, with whipped-cream topping, of course.

❀ ❀ ❀

Bring home a ninety-nine-cent teddy bear. Declare today to be National Hugging Day. Then hug and hug again and again.

❀ ❀ ❀

Ask friends and relatives to save copies of hobby magazines he can't afford, then tie them together with a ribbon for a gift that will give many hours of browsing pleasure.

❀ ❀ ❀

Here we grow again! Pick a rosebud or a daisy for his desk. Can you locate a wildflower for his workbench every day this week? Or bring home a flourishing new shrub for the yard. This time your note could say, "My love for you is growing every day" or "Grow old along with me; the best is yet to be."

❀ ❀ ❀

Use anything as a first installment that will give a clue to good things coming up:

- A floor plan of the dream house you picked together along with a bank book showing a record of your first deposit toward the down payment.
- A small shovel as your promise to go camping with him even though he knows you don't care for the wild side of life.
- One woman, short on money but long on dreams, tied her meaningful handmade card to a brand-new seventy-five-cent brick with the message, "This is the first installment on the brick fireplace I am saving for by working extra Saturday hours." Still looking forward to keeping her promise on his birthday six months later, she had a load of firewood delivered to let him know she hadn't forgotten. The day the fireplace was finally installed, she was ready with a big banner tacked to the mantle: "Ready, Aim, . . . Fire!"
- A package of seeds for flowers that attract hummingbirds, a humming-

bird feeder, and a gallon of liquid food.
- Tickets to the local high school or college football game and a McDonald's gift certificate for use afterward.
- Male and female puppies. He plans to breed them, of course.
- A fancy basket full of his favorite snacks to enjoy while he watches the World Series or Super Bowl on television. Baby Ruth candy bars? Bubble gum with baseball cards enclosed? Doughnuts and cider?

❀ ❀ ❀

Give him a wild tie, maybe one that tells a story of the two of you, like horses because you love to ride together or sea horses because a sea horse pin was his first gift to you.

With a touch of candor and a dash of cheeky wit, one long-married wife who loves to tease her hubby about old girlfriends gave him a tie that simply says, "I'm Married" to wear to his high school reunion. With a friendly wink she told him in a flattering tone, "A handsome husband like you needs it for protection."

❀ ❀ ❀

Write him a love letter or poem in calligraphy. Inspire your correspondence by taking a peek at chapter 1 in this book.

❀ ❀ ❀

Does he have difficulty remembering special occasions? Not to worry. Make up a personalized desk or wall calendar by writing in dates as gentle reminders for family birthdays, anniversaries, and other important happenings. Include upcoming events like Secretary's Day, graduations, your church's homecoming, a reunion with navy buddies, or his godparents' fiftieth wedding reaffirmation ceremony. Attach a master list to show everything at a glance.

❀ ❀ ❀

Select and address a box of appropriate greeting cards. Include stamps, and on the upper right corner of the envelopes, pencil in the date of the occasion to help him remember when to send each card. Kids will be especially surprised receiving cards from Dad.

❈ ❈ ❈

Tape his favorite television program, then give it as a surprise gift.

❈ ❈ ❈

You and the kids can autograph a large photo of yourselves, then cut it into jigsaw pieces. Mail your photo puzzle to his office. Coworkers likely will have fun helping assemble the pieces. If you add a frame, cardboard, and paste, he may get it all together to show off his fantastic family atop the desk.

❈ ❈ ❈

All year, clip out weird or funny headlines or interesting stories from newspapers and magazines about his favorite subjects like golf, tennis, or deer hunting. Toss in a couple of pertinent articles on bedroom life or raising kids or canning vegetables or whatever the two of you are into right now. Scribble on your very own comments to stir up a few giggles and paste everything in an album.

❈ ❈ ❈

For a nostalgic gift that lasts through times that change, assemble old love letters sent to each other years ago in an album.

❁ ❁ ❁

When you go alone to the old hometown
to visit relatives, snap photographs of the
first house you two bought so he can have
the satisfaction of seeing how beautifully
the bushes and shrubs and trees he so
carefully planted have grown and what
improvements like porches or outbuild-
ings other owners have added over the
years. A few pictures of the high school
where you met, favorite dating spots, and
the new mall outside of town will be
appreciated, too.

❁ ❁ ❁

Cross-stitch and frame his favorite quota-
tion, joke, or Bible verse.

❁ ❁ ❁

Make him feel special by having an
engraved nameplate made for the door
of his hobby room or workshop, or
frame one that you have cross-stitched.
Personalize a beach towel, sweater,
his shorts, handkerchiefs, or shirt pockets and cuffs by embroidering his initials.

❀ ❀ ❀

Make a cardboard mood chart with clocklike hands so he can signal everybody how he is feeling today. Let him know he can post the chart on the door when he feels:

- The need to be alone until noon
- Worried
- The need to talk
- Grumpy, grouchy
- The need for some TLC
- Excited
- Content
- Happy

❀ ❀ ❀

Promise coupons that meet a special need or satisfy a wish will speak softly yet say so much. I promise:

- a free window washing for all eighteen windows in the house.
- a massage at five-thirty after a tough day at work.
- an afternoon of peace and quiet from the phone and kids and plenty of popcorn and potato chips on any Saturday during the football season.

- to keep the lawn mowed for you during September.
- to stop nagging about your weight.
- to walk the dog twice daily during your birthday week.

GIFTS FOR PREGNANT FATHERS

❀ ❀ ❀

A waiting-room kit to be used during delivery countdown. For reading, include a couple of his favorite magazines and some food for thought, a small Bible with encouraging Scriptures highlighted. Don't forget small change for the telephone, a list of phone numbers of folks who will want to know delivery-room details afterward, snacks, cigars, or lollipops to hand out, and a few appropriate cartoons and poems or quotations about babies and pregnancy that poke fun at the frustrations, fears, and foibles of new parents.

❀ ❀ ❀

A drawerful of brightly wrapped little packages "For the Fabulous Father of Our New Baby," which you have purchased in the months before the birthing. These will be opened as marked after Baby arrives (Day 1, Day 2, Day 3, etc.).

- Says Beth, "After our first baby, we joked about the 'baby drift,' the distance we both felt between us because so much of our time, attention, and energy was focused on getting our new son settled into a routine. The fourteen days of surprise packages were my private preplanned campaign of love and assurance to remind him that he remained my first priority, even though it didn't seem like it right then."

- From Terry: "The gift my husband liked most was my personal love letter to him thanking him for making me a mother once again and listing the ways I felt that we really would shine as parents."

5

Little "Thinks" Mean a Lot

Small kindnesses are kindnesses, too, and every bit as sacred

We cannot do a kindness too soon, because we never know how soon it will be too late.

UNKNOWN

The great acts of love are done by those who habitually perform small acts of thoughtfulness. Small kindnesses are kindnesses, too, and every bit as sacred and holy.

One busy schoolteacher-wife and mother of four said, "I know I shouldn't take the old flame for granted, but I don't have much money or time to fuss like some do. Besides, it's hard to break through my macho man's stern upbringing with new ideas that may bring out strong sentiments and emotions that he's not used to admitting even to himself."

Often those things that count the most don't take much time or cash. Besides, even the most immovable males cannot resist warmhearted gestures intended to meet their needs on the spot. Throwing in a load of his laundry, or delivering an unexpected frosty glass of ginger ale when he is in the middle of repairing a cranky chain saw, or helping him assemble an ensemble for the first day of a new job can move life out of the ordinary realm. Small tokens of love like this often send high-voltage "I care" messages that are bound to warm the most distant of hearts.

The magic generated by everyday acts of kindness can make life together worthwhile, even though your pockets are almost empty, you are behind on the mortgage, and your toddler needs his tonsils removed before the company health insurance coverage kicks in. And, remembered later, these loving acts can sustain a relationship through touchy or tumultuous times.

Never in a million years could you put to use all of the ideas that follow; many will not even fit your life. But every now and then you can try out one or two to add a smile to your relationship.

*May you always be doing those good, kind things
that show you are a child of God, for this will
bring much praise and glory to the Lord.*

PHILIPPIANS 1:11, TLB

□ One woman's story: "Bruce lost his
job. Bills went unpaid. The kids' ortho-
dontist was dismissed. There was no
new dress for my mom's funeral, so I
wore what I had. When I was feeling
really low one day, Bruce brought
home one yellow rose, my favorite. In
a few days, after returning from a dis-
couraging job interview, he left
another rose in a vase on the kitchen
table. When one wilted, another
appeared in its place. I objected and
told Bruce that our budget simply
would not allow frivolities.

"'Flowers always make a good day,'
he said. I knew he was right. My wonderful guy explained that just because
everything in our lives wasn't perfect
didn't mean we couldn't enjoy ourselves. Bruce still doesn't have a job,
but usually we have a fresh yellow rose
on the table anyway. Sometimes I am
the one who digs around in the bottom

of my purse or wallet or down into the depths of the recliner rocker looking for fallen change. When I find it, I fly off to the local discount florist. I think it lets Bruce know that I believe in him, no matter what.

"This one little effort has raised the morale of our whole family during this difficult time of unemployment and has had a calming effect. Even the kids have become Dad's cheerleaders by picking a daisy or dandelion to stick in the 'high hopes' vase now and then. The sunny spot on the kitchen table helps us remember we are all in this struggle together and reminds us how glad we are for each other. Those flowers will remain a part of our lives no matter how tight things get."

❀ ❀ ❀

Humor his little quirks. Remind yourself often that we all have crazy habits from hand-me-down genes or leftovers from our bringing up. Maybe his father was a lawyer and he likes order (and nothing but) in his home. If he believes all the drinking glasses in the cupboard should match exactly or that all the shirts in the closet should face south, then appreciate his eye for perfection. Can it hurt to put in a nice new set of tumblers or turn the shirt hangers around? Remind yourself that that's the kind of neat partner who also picks up his own socks!

Is he from New York, but now your home is in Alabama? Spurn the southern standards of the past and declare "Gone with the Grits" week, even if your Mississippi mother would raise eyebrows of disapproval.

If it pleases him to sleep on the west side of the bed, why not? Little things count.

❀ ❀ ❀

Encourage his interests. Agree to be his co-pilot and chief traffic navigator to help locate a hunting-and-fishing store downtown in a big, busy city. Go with him to a war movie or to a boat show and plan to enjoy as much of it as you can. Love breeds love. Bet he'll be more willing to make some minor accommodations for you sometime up ahead!

❀ ❀ ❀

Appreciate the results of your talented man's hobbies. Frame and hang the family photo he took with his new camera. Peptalk the new buds on his favorite house plants and bring home fertilizer spikes when you shop. Stir up a batch of chili sauce from the tomatoes he brings in from the garden.

❁ ❁ ❁

On his birthday, secretly send his mom and dad a card or flowers, thanking them for birthing this good guy. You can be sure he will hear about it sooner or later. Smile.

Bonus idea: Write a letter to each of his parents, thanking them for instilling the good character traits in him that you most admire: dependability, honesty, love for family and home, respect for self and others, personal cleanliness, or whatever. Thank them for sacrificing so he could finish college and make a good living for your family and for giving him an appreciation for the good things in life like art or classical music or uplifting inspirational books.

❁ ❁ ❁

Show your love for him by sending his parents a card or note now and then when they face particular challenges like retirement or separation from children or grandchildren, grief over death of friends and relatives their own age or even of a beloved pet. You can also let them know that the two of you care when they are enduring things like chronic illness or an adverse farming season because of drought. And don't forget notes of encouragement to the caregiver if one is ill. Most men want to keep in touch with parents but feel they are not very good at it.

❀ ❀ ❀

If his parents live in your city, he will be pleased if you stop by occasionally to ask what you can do for them. Run an errand? Call a family meeting to help with a difficult decision? Take one of them to the doctor? If parents live far away, let them know when they can expect regular phone calls, then remind him to call or do it yourself. Even if your relationship isn't close with his mom and dad, a little creative attention will make their lives brighter and your marriage a little more solid.

□ One new mother, overwhelmed by the demands of her infant daughter, felt separated from her husband because of weariness and lack of time together. Her solution? On separate slips of paper, she listed small kindnesses she knew she could do for him that would show her love and placed them in a crystal bowl on the dining room table. He was asked to draw one every morning before work. "He definitely looks forward each evening to little things like a back rub or a favorite movie I have rented, and these small things give a feeling of connectedness, even as we adjust to the busyness of new parenthood," she says. "My 'postpartum labor pains' were eased a bit, too, when he suggested that, beginning Sunday, I get to draw from the crystal bowl, too!"

❀ ❀ ❀

See the doctor for an annual mammogram just because he asks, or give up smoking or some other habit he dislikes. You know he cares about you and your health. Be sure to tell him why you are making the effort.

❀ ❀ ❀

Touch him and ask how he feels today, especially if he has been sick or feeling down lately.

❀ ❀ ❀

Mail birthday and anniversary cards to
him on time. Now and then, save an especially meaningful one he sent to you, and
return it to him with a note telling how
much it meant and why. Maybe the two of
you can keep a note or naughty card going
back and forth for a while. Small secret
maneuvers like this pack a powerful
"punch" for your relationship.

❀ ❀ ❀

Reminisce together. Rehash intimate
events in the enchanting history of your
life together that are mysteries to the rest
of the world. When you move away from
the hometown, talk about how it was when
you brought your firstborn home from the
hospital to the upstairs bedroom on Summer Street. When you sell your seven-year-
old car, recall aloud the kids' backseat
excitement when you all piled in to drive a
shiny new Ford out of the showroom and
how you stopped for root-beer floats on
the way home. Such happy times are little
love connections that enhance the joy of
your lives together.

❀ ❀ ❀

Tell the kids in front of your mate that the
two of you are together for good, that your
love for him never wavers, even if you
argue sometimes.

❀ ❀ ❀

Build him up in front of others, especially
the kids. On the way to church, point out
that he spent two hours washing and vacuuming the car yesterday. Looks nice, huh?
Say so. He's sure to feel flattered if you
remember to show off his oil paintings and
hand-carved Christmas figurines when
company comes.

❀ ❀ ❀

Ask a few questions like, What are your
needs? How can I help meet them? How
can I please you more? Are there areas of
our life that need talking about? What are
they? Have him write a winter wish list.
Bet he asks you to do the same.

❀ ❀ ❀

Love enough to respect the other's inde-
pendence. Better to stay out of the bathroom when the door is closed. Never

snoop through his things or open his mail or monitor his phone calls. Allowing the other's privacy says, "I trust you. I don't need to know all about everything in your life, because you are perfectly capable of running it." If dust and dirt get out of hand and you must invade his office or other personal place periodically to clean up, let him know beforehand.

❦ ❦ ❦

Keeping old addresses, phone numbers, or photos of pleasant times spent with a previous "significant other" can become a major heartache or annoyance because these things tend to destroy oneness. Removing little reminders of a previous marriage or heavy relationship lets him know that your love is permanently his.

❦ ❦ ❦

Nothing destroys trust faster than betraying a confidence. Your mother does not need to know if your husband wears a support for his hernia or that he decided to color his hair, and what good would it do to tell his friends that alcoholism runs in his family? Sometimes "Keep my secrets" is only implied, but secrecy is sweet, if kept.

❀ ❀ ❀

Find humorous ways to remind him of a job you need him to do, or that he has promised to do. Leave a note where he'll find it when he's not stressed. Some ideas:

- I'll let you warm your feet on me in bed if you'll get that heartworm pill down Fluffy sometime today.
- I'll swap my piece of chocolate pie for a night out with you. We've both been working too hard lately.

❀ ❀ ❀

Did he forget your anniversary again? Embroider a necktie with the date.

❀ ❀ ❀

If he (inadvertently, of course) gets a little overzealous in conversation with Miss Wonderful at a party, embroider a plain necktie with the words "I'm Married." Then gently remind him that it is for wearing at any and all future parties when she will be in attendance.

▢ Says Marnie: "Some points of conten-
tion may be better tossed off as mere
trifles or queer quirks rather than
labeled infirmities. A few things
never will be different simply because
the other one doesn't see the value of
change. Jim gets his own Sunday
night supper but always forgets to
wipe up the kitchen counter, although
I have asked and asked. I finally con-
cluded that quietly doing that little
task myself wouldn't take more than
forty-five minutes out of my entire
life. Later, in a month when I forgot
to fill the car gas tank for the fifth
time and Jim pretended not to notice,
I was reminded of the wisdom of a
forgiving attitude. We both mean
well."

❀ ❀ ❀

Learn to tiptoe around life's crazy times
with a little preplanning. A wise wife says,
"My husband has been recuperating from
minor surgery and the sadness of a recent
death in the family. As usual, our rambunc-
tious kids are ready to climb all over him
when he comes in the door exhausted.

Since I get home ahead and have time to recover, I thought it would be a good idea to have our two preschoolers occupied in small ways. Sometimes, I take our sons for a late-afternoon romp in the park to work off pent-up energy. Bill has told me several times how very much he appreciates having the house to himself for a little while after exhausting days at work."

❀ ❀ ❀

Compliment his fathering. If you love to see him slam-dunking night after night out in the driveway with your son, say so. If you appreciate him accommodating your seven-year-old's tooth fairy "con game" with his last dollar or tucking her into bed with a story every Sunday night, let him know.

❀ ❀ ❀

Volunteer to tape his favorite sports event from television when he will be occupied doing other things.

❀ ❀ ❀

Surprise him by volunteering to do a despised chore. "I'll take over for a couple of hours while you get out of here," one wife told her out-of-work husband who was spending a frustrating Saturday afternoon mailing resumes. She stepped in to type cover letters and address envelopes, drive the kids to baseball practice, take the car to be washed or for new brakes, weed the garden, call his sister, or return his books to the library.

❀ ❀ ❀

If you know that he needs several late nights to catch up in the office, pack a survival kit to help him tough it out. Include packets of instant coffee and cream, crackers with jam and peanut butter, fruit, boxed drinks, nuts, or other favorite snacks. You'll probably be asleep when he returns, so include a note that promises a favorite dessert in the refrigerator when he gets home or a "good night" (whatever that means to the two of you) when things get back to normal.

> ❑ Joe and I are on different schedules. I arrive home from my teaching job after he leaves for work for the three-to-eleven shift. It has been hard, but we need our jobs to save for a down

payment on a house. One night, when I got to the house just after four, I distinctly heard Joe's voice, though I knew he had to be at work. "It's me, beloved buddy. I love you and I want you to know." My wonderful guy had prepared a message on tape timed to start just after I got home. Joe was reminding me that next year at this time we would be in our new house and we could think about working fewer hours or changing jobs. I played the tape three times, because I know how much he misses our evenings together. Maybe I will leave a taped love message for him timed to play when he gets up some morning in an empty house.

❀ ❀ ❀

It's been a tough week. A tough month. His nerves seem strained and stretched. Help protect his time so he can relax. Take phone calls and use your wise discretion to refuse less important invitations. Encourage the kids to keep the clamor down when he comes home dead on his feet. Ask how you can protect his private meditation and prayer time.

❊ ❊ ❊

You need plenty of personal privacy to keep your life on an even keel. One smart wife, trying to cope with a full-time office job, housework, and children, frankly expressed to her husband the need for time alone. He agreed to set the coffeepot timer forty-five minutes earlier than usual on workdays. The pleasant coffee aroma now serves as his gentle waker-upper so he can take care of the children's morning needs and start breakfast. She is allowed early time to do whatever she wants. "My day's outlook has changed to positive," she notes. "It's like he is saying to me, 'You are important, too,' and gives me lots more motivation to nurture others in the family."

□ From a New York wife: "Tim and I both hold difficult jobs, but as a teacher, he gets home a couple of hours ahead of me and has time alone. I arrive tired and frazzled after eight hours in a frenzied advertising office and an hour of wrestling with trucks and hot-rodders on the crowded freeway. Our evenings were spent picking at each other; then I finally figured out why. By the time I got home, Tim was refreshed and ready to gab pleasantly. Not me. All I wanted was peace and privacy, complete silence, and sometimes a couple of aspirin. I needed a corner to call my own and some space to hang out by myself.

"After discussing our constant bickering, we agreed that when I come in the front door, I will be forgiven for heading straight for the bedroom for an hour. Sometimes I flop on the bed, sometimes I turn on a CD, and once in a while I soak in the tub. But, when my time is up, I'm a new woman and ready to carry on in a more loving way. Tim calls me 'The Comeback Kid.' Our squabbles have stopped, and our conversation is more sharing. My resentment has plummeted. This is such a simple solution that we wondered why it had taken so long."

❀ ❀ ❀

Oneness created here! Purposely taking time to break away for good conversation with your partner is not often thought of as a kindness. But good talk is not only a gracious way to say "I love you," but also a connecting point after being separated all day or all week. The two of you are a pretty good team, so after a week of worry or the constant tension of living with the gift and grind of kids, give yourselves a chance to regroup. Suggest a long walk or a snack 'n' yak time together on the back deck, or listen to CDs together when teens are off to a Friday-night football game. If necessary, start a new policy of earlier bedtime for the younger children (even if it means using ploys like, "You can stay awake as long as you like if you are reading in bed"). The two of you can talk through concerns and glow over shared happinesses without distraction.

❀ ❀ ❀

Try not to interrupt when he is reading or concentrating. Perhaps what you have to say can wait until later.

❀ ❀ ❀

Issue a Veto Coupon that allows the love of your life to skip attending a hated event like the annual Christmas party at your office, your high school reunion, the ballet, putting up curtains in the new house, department store shopping, or your daughter's last school band concert of the year. He can simply redeem the escape coupon to get out of the occasion gracefully. Your part is to handle the event without him or to make tactful excuses and just stay home too.

❀ ❀ ❀

Push the covers close in around him when you get up first for an early morning jog. A few tender tucks feel so good!

PAMPER EACH OTHER

One wife of thirty years told me, "Something mellow and wonderful happens when we serve or pamper each other in small ways as energy allows." She shares her "little thinks":

❀ ❀ ❀

If you are at home, make it a point to step over and unlock the back door for him five minutes before he is expected so he won't have to put down briefcase or tool box or packages and fumble for keys.

❀ ❀ ❀

If you are driving, unlock and hold open the passenger's door for him first, then walk around and get in the car yourself.

❀ ❀ ❀

Stow away safety equipment in his car — things like flares and flashlight, blanket and extra jacket, small shovel for snow, and perhaps a little sack of gravel for help on icy roads. Maybe they will never be needed, maybe only once, but providing them will show "intensive care" on your part.

❀ ❀ ❀

Have the covers turned back at bedtime. If you share an electric blanket with dual controls, don't forget to preheat his side of the bed, too.

❀ ❀ ❀

When you know he is homeward bound after a long and exhausting day, prepare a hot bubble bath for a long, steaming soak.

Or lay out towels and reading matter and get the whirlpool churning. Ahh!

❀ ❀ ❀

Update his Rolodex cards or address book, just because he will probably never get around to it.

❀ ❀ ❀

Do your part to keep the checkbook balanced and the car gas tank full.

❀ ❀ ❀

Surprise him with a gourmet meal for two now and then. Serve with candlelight.

❀ ❀ ❀

Warm up his car and scrape the windshield once in a while on frosty mornings when you do your own.

❀ ❀ ❀

See that he gets the Sunday funnies or sports pages first. Yes, even before the kids!

❀ ❀ ❀

Return things to the store for him. Most men hate doing this.

❀ ❀ ❀

How old is he? "I always put thirty-nine candles on his cake in the shape of a question mark," says Lonnie. "Nobody has to know his exact age, especially since he looks ten years younger."

❀ ❀ ❀

Small burdens may loom large in an already frustratingly overcrowded life. Maybe the Little League team he coaches came in last. Is he struggling with painful bunions or poison ivy or an allergic rash? Laughter heals. Send a humorous greeting card that makes light of an annoying situation. There are plenty of cards out there to bring smiles into nearly any event.

> ❑ From Ellen: "I try not to ask my man to take up my private projects. If duty calls me to play Good Samaritan and pick up an elderly lady for church, but he doesn't feel like it, I have learned to forget it. Some Sunday ahead when I will be making the run by myself may be a better bet. A good alternative has been to take my older friend out to lunch for some

good old-fashioned woman talk when my husband is out of town."

LOOK AND *DO* TOUCH!

Sadly, many couples who have been married a long time stop touching except when one or the other has sex in mind. Blitz him with hugs and kisses. Such outright displays say to him, "I'm glad you're you." They show that you love him just because he exists. One psychologist surprised a lot of people with results of a poll that showed that men crave affection (of all things!) from their woman more than any other single thing. And women? They want affirmation and appreciation. Both want closeness and touching. You may not be the Huxtables, and maybe your family wasn't very affectionate or "touchy feely," but you can copy small satisfying acts of physical love that other couples shared with us:

❀ ❀ ❀

Even if you are not a morning person, you can give an uncomplicated good-morning hug or a friendly light touch as he passes by in pajamas, coffee cup in hand.

*Surprise him with a gourmet meal for two now
and then. Serve with candlelight.*

❀ ❀ ❀

Come back through the front door for a second good-bye hug, or turn back one more time and blow a kiss. Don't forget to catch any and all kisses blown your way.

❀ ❀ ❀

Put an arm around him or give him a shoulder hug as you stand in a bank or theater line together. Squeeze hands while holding hands for the table blessing or after praying together. Seal it with a smile and a quick kiss.

❀ ❀ ❀

Kindred spirits like the two of you can stroke an arm or cheek when kind words are said. Be sure to make eye contact, too.

❀ ❀ ❀

You can briefly stop and massage the back of the other's neck when you pass behind, no sensuality involved. Nibble your partner's ear or sit on each other's laps. Tweak noses. Nobody else will notice if you cuddle close in the church pew or at a concert.

❀ ❀ ❀

Long, long hugs with a little back stroking and no sex demands can do a lot to satisfy the urge for closeness and the "skin starved" dissatisfaction that most everyone is said by psychologists to experience. Hug long, even though your parents didn't do it that way. Hug just as long as the other seems to want to. If your mate is a short-term hugger, let him know that you need more.

❀ ❀ ❀

Hold hands when you cross the street or walk from the car into a public building or when you pray together. Touch knees under the table with a knowing look or plop down next to him for a wild rock in the double hammock or catch some country breezes in the porch glider.

GET SOME GOOD TALK GOING

One counselor said a woman came to the office in shock, stating, "My husband is leaving me. He told me when he came home from work yesterday that our marriage had gotten drab, boring, lifeless, and hopeless, and that he had found a one-room apartment. Sure, we've both been too busy to sit down and talk much lately, but I was absolutely stunned. It seemed to me everything had been going fine. What happened?"

Your marriage may not need to be rescued from the brink of divorce, but small problems turn into big ones and healthy marriages turn sour if there isn't much connecting through good and satisfying conversation or if one or both partners are always guarding their heart from the other. Here's how to encourage more openness:

❀ ❀ ❀

When the dishes are cleared and the kids have settled down to homework, have a second cup of coffee after dinner to share events of the day. Coffee in hand ensures no one will be folding laundry, fiddling with the TV remote, or playing with the dog. Be creative. Continue the coffee connection by bringing the pot into the bedroom or sun room or take chairs out back under the stars. For reasons unknown, low lights often bring out the best conversations.

❀ ❀ ❀

If you can't think of anything particular to
talk about, ask, "What was the best thing
that happened to you today?" Or stun
your partner by requesting a list of five
things he would like done around the
house next month in order of priority.
Promise to get as many done as you can.
Surprise him by doing them all!

❀ ❀ ❀

Ask him what changes can be made to
improve your relationship and make him
happier. That will get his attention! Some
of the changes may not be in your power,
but you can agree to do a few things or
whatever you can, even if it takes real
effort. Just asking lets him know how
important he is to you and is bound to generate conversation.

❀ ❀ ❀

Your Prince Charming may not feel so
charming today. Perhaps his few words
seem sharper than usual and you feel
cheated. Can you find out why he's having
such a rough time? Your "little think" for
tonight may be simply responding to his

mood with understanding. The peaceful haven you have provided after a long day is a wonderful gift. If you sense his need to share, you can say something like, "You're extra quiet tonight. Want to tell me what is on your mind?" or "I feel like there's something we should be praying about. I'm willing." Sometimes just a hand on the shoulder or a quick kiss gives a powerful message of understanding, no words needed.

Are There Any Lovers out There?

A happy marriage—or a strong faith— doesn't kill sensuality

> *For these few years, H. and I feasted on love,*
> *every mode of it—solemn and merry, romantic*
> *and realistic, sometimes as dramatic as a*
> *thunderstorm, sometimes as comfortable and*
> *unemphatic as putting on your soft slippers. No*
> *cranny of heart or body remained unsatisfied.*

C. S. LEWIS, recalling intimate life with his wife

How's your love life?

Some more demure and diehard critics have asked why I include this rather racy chapter. Why all the sizzling sexual expressions of love (even if presented in wholesome good taste and in a lighthearted way)? The glow in marriage dims for many reasons. Keeping sexuality and sensual pleasure alive and well, fun, and getting better every day plays a major role in maintaining a forever kind of love. A happy marriage doesn't kill an active imagination. Neither does faith in God.

Dr. James Dobson noted in *Focus on the Family* magazine: "We must work to protect 'what God has joined together' with all the creativity and compassion we can pour into it. That's done (in part) by taking time for romantic activities despite pressing obligations and overcommitted schedules."

One husband writes: "At various times, our lives are too crazy or too ordinary or too busy. The daily routine of kids, chores, car pools, stressful jobs, and even a terrible health trauma has 'set in' like solid cement. Sometimes we feel so separated. But good sex play reestablishes something wonderful between us, and we really do become one flesh all over again, as the Bible says a man and his wife should be. We get new courage to go on."

The counseling world seems overloaded with sex manuals from well-meaning therapists who, some contend, have the worst marriage record of almost any profession, and from researchers who present sterile national statistics that compare us to the "national norm," whatever that is. Television talk-show hosts dispense pop psychology before millions of viewers, pursuing the shallow depths of the psyches of their sometimes less-than-inspiring guests. New Age thinkers write books with wild and woolly ideas that are gobbled up as if they contain the wisdom of the ages. Maybe we need more sensible, down-to-earth sex stuff like the ideas in this chapter, plucked straight from the lives of men and women in mostly healthy relationships who are willing to allow us an inside look. Here, loving couples share "eclectic and electric" suggestions that have made their loving more frolicsome, more playful, and more joyful.

So, hang on to your hats (and possibly each other). This chapter is a supermarket of raucous, healthy, and hardy little prescriptions that can help bring back some of the feelings of sensual frolicking, romping, teasing, playing, pretending, and surprising one another—those same pleasures that you likely felt during your very first years together. If some of these suggestions sound slightly bawdy or brash, well then, stop blushing and go off somewhere to write your very own guilt guide. Marriage is meant to be enjoyed, and sex is half the fun. With carefully laid plans to make some of these dreams come true, the precious little people who live in your house happily can be borrowed by your best buddy or off at Grandma's or at camp or spending an overnight with their friends so that you and your spouse can spend time alone.

Note: Choose only those ideas that fit you and your mate, and no fair telling around the office watercooler tomorrow!

❀ ❀ ❀

Contrive a secret signal that means "Let's":

- Quietly place a rose on his pillow.
- Paste a smile sticker on the front of the refrigerator.
- Suggest a game of strip poker.
- Embroider a throw pillow with a huge exclamation point or with the words "In the Mood" to be turned right side up in your bedroom on promising nights.

- Have a favorite love song playing on the stereo as he comes in the door.
- Hang an appropriate sign on the bedroom door. Ideas:

  - Couples Retreat Here Tonight
  - Handsome Man Welcome Inside
  - Free Massage Parlor. Come On In
  - Welcome to the Midnight Club
  - Baby Maybe?

❀ ❀ ❀

Since tonight will definitely *not* be "business as usual," fire up his metabolism by calling every hour at his place of business to tell him so.

❀ ❀ ❀

Let the rest of the world *tsk-tsk* themselves to death. You are sick of looking at each other over a dinner table that includes a high chair, sticky fingers, and conversations about scraped knees and whether or not the Little League team came out on top last night. Send an invitation to his office for a private Wednesday evening at home, no children allowed (you will swap babysitting with a neighbor and turn your kids over to her tonight). Make a big deal of marking the event plainly on his wall calendar with a red pencil or maybe stick on a heart. Ask if he can think of something special to do, then plan ahead together. Or give him a blank "Mirth and Madness" coupon for March 21 and ask him to fill in three activities. You will arrive home prepared with the big size of Keri massage lotion and a new CD, then attach a front doorknob hanger that says Love-In Tonight. The sign on the bedroom door says Private. Make it a point to unplug the phones and pull the shades. Other activities? Censored.

❧ ❧ ❧

Stick an intimate promise message suitable for his eyes only inside a Chinese fortune cookie or bake it inside a cupcake. Excuse the kids for their dessert in front of the television so the two of you will be by yourselves to enjoy your sensuous sweet treat with a favorite espresso drink.

❧ ❧ ❧

Cut out a red cardboard Sex Chip to be cashed in "as needed." Place it in a sealed envelope on his desk. Or have it sent to his hotel room when he is staying out of town for a few days. He'll bring it home with great expectation. Better yet, could you appear on the hotel scene unexpectedly to make sure he cashes his chip in promptly and correctly?

❀ ❀ ❀

Hand him an envelope of lovemaking certificates, one terrific idea written on each. Allow him to pick one. Here's your chance to make dream fantasies come true.

❀ ❀ ❀

When he comes in the door, dress up, up, up or down, down, down. Explain that it's your new alive-after-five look.

❀ ❀ ❀

If you are out together at a restaurant, play footsie under the table for a while, then whisper, "Let's get out of here and see what we can cook up at home."

❀ ❀ ❀

Have a trail of confetti laid from the back door to the bedroom when he comes in. Romance your space with a trail of lighted candles, paper valentine doilies, fragrant incense, or your own lingerie. Men notice that sort of thing.

❀ ❀ ❀

If he gets home before you do, leave a seductive message on the answering machine that outlines your full intentions.

❀ ❀ ❀

When he comes in the back door and calls, "I'm home!" holler, "I am, too! Come find me." You, of course, have had time to make the transformation from Mom to Greta Gorgeous and are waiting in the bubble bath (this move is well planned!). You need someone to dry you off.

❀ ❀ ❀

When you hear his shower running before bedtime, stand outside the curtain and tell him you are offering valet service this evening, then have hot towels ready when he steps out. Better yet, remind him that saving water is important in these days of environmental concern. Then step in with him. He'll get the picture, and you'll both be squeaky clean.

❀ ❀ ❀

Have his bathroom laid out some evening just like they do in model homes with two stemmed glasses, his and hers lingerie, matching monogrammed washcloths and towels, talcum, heart- or petal-shaped soap, fragrant lotions and potions, and lighted candles. For an extra, dramatic touch, you can always dress up like Marie the Maid and make sure all his needs are taken care of.

❀ ❀ ❀

On his birthday, or any day, send a half-dozen red roses to his office "from a secret admirer." Let the secretaries' tongues wag. Your note will read, "I'm not that sort of girl, but . . ." Later, when he walks in the door, you can ask, in the usual way, "Anything special happen today?" His answer should provide some very interesting conversation and maybe, just maybe, he will get your sweet drift.

❀ ❀ ❀

Pretend. Pretend. Pretend. Tonight your name is Ruby Red and he is your drop-dead gorgeous guy. Or could you be

Scarlett for an evening? Can he be Rhett? Bogey and Bacall? Could you make merry by becoming a "Scanty Santy" in your designer suit at Christmas? Think about it.

❀ ❀ ❀

Men's night out (and he'll never have to leave home): Here's your chance to show off all those pretty teddies and bikinis and black underwear, the beautiful ones with the scratchy lace that have been lying in the back of the drawer. You can be a runway model for this private trunk showing or provide some giggles by becoming a walking fashion violation. Add some class to your fashion show by playing perfect background music and offer a Polaroid camera for instantaneous recording of the events. Bet he'll do a double take! When he gives chase, be sure you allow yourself to get caught.

❀ ❀ ❀

When he comes in from the daily rat race, report that the electric power went out this afternoon and that the two of you will need to spend the evening at home with only candles to light your night. After serving your well-planned sumptuous candle-light dinner, ask if he can think of something to do (maybe some "hands on" activities) since television and reading the newspaper are out of the question. Whether he can or can't think of anything, serve your luscious heart-shaped cheesecake or a giant cookie (the one with the *Let's* message on top) for dessert. Or offer red-hot cinnamon candy "pills" after dinner and tell him they were prescribed by Dr. Ruth to take effect in thirty minutes. The candles will flicker, the room will become darker, then—well, that's your business.

❊ ❊ ❊

Have a helium balloon delivered with instructions for him to pop it. Your message is tucked inside: "Sack-In for Two at 29 Elm Street beginning at seven o'clock tonight." Offer a money-back certificate, guaranteeing satisfaction.

❊ ❊ ❊

Just tell him plainly, "I love you. I need you. I can't live without you. Snuggling in bed sounds good to me tonight."

❀ ❀ ❀

Present him with the key to a swank hotel
room you rented for the night. Tell him the
festivities begin at seven — and offer to
drive.

❀ ❀ ❀

Set out a photo of yourself along with a
small card on which you have hand printed
in calligraphy, "Turn me on!" Or parade
through the house carrying a jumbo cardboard key. When he asks why, tell him.

❀ ❀ ❀

Winter warmer: On a cold night, just say
to him, "I turned on the electric blanket
and I've even heated up a bottle of massage lotion just in case." Tell him that you
are "a soft touch."

❀ ❀ ❀

Wrap your love in ribbons. You have had
this same good and gentle lover for all
twelve years (or however long) you've
been wed, right? Give your partner a
dozen yards of romantic satin-and-lace ribbon, one yard for each year you've been
happily married, and tell him that you are

"fit to be tied tonight." The trendy title of your game? "Houdini," of course! Directions? "Handle with your usual loving imagination and tender care." Now reverse roles, just for fun.

❋ ❋ ❋

Suggest a his-and-hers shopping trip together to prepare a pretty wardrobe for your "Saturday Night Special." Remind him what wise and witty Dorothy Parker said: "Brevity is the soul of lingerie."

❋ ❋ ❋

Alternate plan: Tonight, home shopping is on your schedule. Order a lingerie catalog or some other intimate fun catalog and plan to flop on the bed with a tray of snacks and marking pencils so the two of you can giggle while selecting favorites. To make sure of correct sizes, you will be double-checking each other's measurements all over with a tape measure. Maybe you'll never order, maybe you will. . . .

❋ ❋ ❋

Make up your own surprise cassette tape to stick in his Sony Walkman. Promise the moon after dark tonight. Tell him you need some bodywork. Can he help out? Let him know how. Your star stud will be blushing when he returns from his early morning jog.

❧ ❧ ❧

Stick provocative notes on packages of jawbreakers or candy bars and leave them in obvious places.

❧ ❧ ❧

Whisper loving suggestions in his ear or scribble them on paper and leave them where only he will see them. Not all ideas will come from the intellectual side of you, of course.

❧ ❧ ❧

Wake him with a massage and kisses.

❧ ❧ ❧

Get published. You and your partner can write your own private handbook for sexual success. Now, don't be fuddy-duddies. Your *Every Couple's Guide* can reap unexpected (and spontaneous) royalties of a different kind as the two of you have fun

reading your manuscript masterpiece
aloud later.

❀ ❀ ❀

Flop on the bed together and make up
your own funky and fictional love story.
Start with: "Vera and John [that's the two
of you] got married, and . . ." He will add
an ending, then an unfinished next sen-
tence. Now you do the same. Make your
lines sensuous and silly or erotic and crazy.

❀ ❀ ❀

Reminisce. Remember how it was when
you first got serious about each other? All
those *feelings?* The wonder of looking deep
into each other's eyes when you first fell in
love? The dreams and fantasies? What did
you think being married would be like
back then? Prop up in bed and reinvent it
all. What were your dreams? What put the
brakes on them? Relive the best love
scenes. You haven't changed all that much,
have you? Let your spouse know if your
feelings now run deeper and better or
what wonderful new things you have discovered about him that you never knew
years ago.

❀ ❀ ❀

Pillow talk: While propped up side by side
in bed, recall your most romantic past
times together. Now is the time to say
things every happily married man or
woman wants to hear:

- I plan to stay married forever, don't you?
- I'm glad I married you. We're right
  for each other.
- Who has more fun than we do?
- Can I have a replay of that one?
- I love you better than anybody.
- Let's _____
  (you fill in the blank).

❀ ❀ ❀

Purposefully discuss the serious side of
sex. Talk about what each of you dreams
about, but never got around to. Ask and
answer questions like, "What do you wish
I would do? Wouldn't do? Show me what
you like best about our intimate times.
How can we make them better?"

❀ ❀ ❀

Taking care of business in an unusual way:
Ann packed a checkered tablecloth,

French bread, a roll of hard sausage, a knife, and drinks, massage lotion, towels, and a blanket for a noonday picnic for two at her lawyer-husband's office. He grinned, got up from his chair, and locked the door when he caught on to what she had in mind. The rest is censored.

❀ ❀ ❀

Leave the suburbs behind and take a picnic to a remote pasture or wooded place with good loving in mind. Or, for a switch, what about a picnic at dusk on the private roof of your duplex apartment building when the neighbors are out of town?

❀ ❀ ❀

How to make a memory together? We don't promise any miracles, but here's how some other longtime couples in love have enhanced the romance behind the closed doors of their bedrooms. Maybe you haven't thought of some of these:

- Spray a little perfume on the sheets, the satin ones.
- Screw a blue light bulb into the bedroom lamp or light candles.

- Make a big deal of having a new dimmer switch installed in the bedroom.
- Redecorate and make your bedroom the most elegant room in the house. Tell him how special that room is to you.
- Music! Music! Music! Tape your own favorite love songs from the radio or play best CD's. Note: A tape player with auto reverse play insures several hours of uninterrupted background music. You wouldn't want to get up to turn over the tape, would you?

❀ ❀ ❀

Head to bed to relax, cuddle, and take turns reading love poems aloud to each other (did you write one?) or read a book that matches your mellow mood. Suggestions: *For Lovers Only* (Hundreth Century, 1991), a guide to love and intimacy; *Love, A Book of Poetry* (Andrews & McMeel, 1992); and *A Vow of Love* (Andrews & McMeel, 1992), an anthology of writings and photographs that evoke romance in many moods.

❀ ❀ ❀

Read together Song of Songs, chapters 5 and 7, from the Bible. Here is a sample:

My lover is radiant and ruddy, outstanding among ten thousand. His head is purest gold; his hair is wavy and black as a raven. His eyes are like doves by the water's streams, washed in milk, mounted like jewels. His cheeks are like beds of spice yielding perfume. His lips are like lilies dripping with myrrh. His arms are rods of gold set with chrysolite. His body is like polished ivory decorated with sapphires. His legs are pillars of marble set on bases of pure gold. His appearance is like Lebanon, choice as its cedars. His mouth is sweetness itself (5:10-16).

TAKE YOUR LOVE ON THE ROAD!

❀ ❀ ❀

Own a boat? Big splash weekend ahead. I dare you to make marital waves way out in the lake while waiting for a fish to take your hook.

❀ ❀ ❀

Whatever were hot tubs invented for, anyway? Hope you have a board fence all

131

around yours for privacy. Or take a one-hour vacation for two in your very own whirlpool.

> ❑ "My husband was scheduled to leave for a lengthy deer-hunting trip Friday afternoon, so I planned to make Thursday a hot-shot night. I met Big Buck (my pet nickname for this ardent hunter) at the door asking, 'How about dessert *before* supper tonight?' He said he should bathe, so I said I would bathe him. His eyes lit up. I was fully dressed, but after awhile he pulled me in with him! We had so much fun and we never left the bathroom." (From a shy but loving wife who prefers to remain anonymous.)

❀ ❀ ❀

Go far out. On a clear night, shake the wrinkles from that old comforter and toss it on the grass in the backyard with a couple of pillows. This evening, you will be checking for falling stars. Discover Venus or Saturn or maybe a whole new galaxy. Or hold hands on the back deck, look at the moon, and listen to the quiet just because you are crazy about each other. Maybe you can celebrate the next full moon by dipping in your backyard pool at midnight or giggle over a game of Scrabble just because neither of you can sleep.

❀ ❀ ❀

Rent a cozy roomette on a train from New York to Rochester. Enjoy dinner in the diner. Do you know about the beautiful scenery along the Hudson River?

❀ ❀ ❀

Swap your apartment or house with a best friend's to provide new space for a weekend getaway. Promise each other clean sheets and a refrigerator full of important snacks. No cost. No hassle. It will feel like the two of you have sneaked away from the world. Bonus idea: Offer to house-sit some friends' dogs while they are away on vacation.

❀ ❀ ❀

Take advantage of almost any glamorous hotel's weekend room rates and all the amenities—swimming pool, sauna, break-fast in bed. Dance away Saturday night in the ballroom. Nothing is too good for the mother and father of your children.

❀ ❀ ❀

Before he leaves for work in the morning, ask to meet him for lunch at Hotel Wonderful. Rent a room afterward for an extra *lo-o-o-ong* lunch hour.

❀ ❀ ❀

The best thing you can do for your marriage is to get out of town! Spend a night (together, of course) at a romantic and quaint bed-and-breakfast. There will be peace and quiet and a country-style breakfast. Go back upstairs afterward and get your money's worth until checkout time. Most B & B's are in picturesque and out-of-the-way locations.

❀ ❀ ❀

Remember how you used to park and spark before you were married? Is your old spot taken at the old quarry or in the orchard by the lake? Why not find out?

❀ ❀ ❀

Invite him to a progressive dinner at home. There will be gourmet dining, beginning

with hors d'oeuvres at the lace-covered
kitchen table and salad in the den with a
romantic short video to view. The main course
(a red-hot and sassy salsa dish) will be served
by candlelight in the dining room, with music
for dancing. A choice of "desserts" will be
offered in the bedroom. Tell your mate to
expect an "uptown" after-dinner treat right
here at home, then have proper (or improper)
attire laid out on the bed. Offer a sentimental
or romantic movie for viewing while the two
of you are seated on big billowy pillows or a
fat feather comforter thrown on the floor.

❀ ❀ ❀

Is night always your time for loving? A
schedule alteration is in order! Set the
alarm early for any morning shenanigans
you can think of. There's lots of time, so
start the day off slowly by waking him
with tender kisses. There will be leisurely
back rubbing and unhurried cuddling.
Both of you will be smiling all day, and no
one else will know why.

❀ ❀ ❀

For a pleasant change during a sizzlingly
hot summer, schedule a Saturday sunrise

session with breakfast for two on your
very private back deck.

❀ ❀ ❀

Speaking of the back deck . . . on somebody's birthday, why not pander to your
sun addiction by sunbathing in your birthday suits? You'll wonder why nobody ever
thought of such a sensible idea before.
Now, aren't you glad you bought the
basket-weave privacy fence for Fido? Saves
purchasing swimsuits, too. Of course, you
will each need help applying sunscreen
lotions all over, and over, and over. P.S.
Don't forget to shut Fido in the kitchen!

❀ ❀ ❀

Hang a safe play bag at the end of baby's
crib on Friday night so the two of you can
enjoy Saturday morning sleep-ins or love-
ins or whatever you want to call them.
Naming them can be half the fun.

❀ ❀ ❀

Could you two long-married lovebirds rent
a waterbed motel room at Intercourse,
Pennsylvania, or Loveland, Colorado, on
vacation, just to be able to say you did?

There now. You have sneaked a discreet peek into the private lives and bedrooms of a few other committed couples. How's your love life in comparison? Are you overlooking something? If yours is plain vanilla, put aside your puritan cloak and borrow a few of these supercharged ideas to turn it into butterscotch or peach marmalade. Dare you! You're married, aren't you?

NOT TONIGHT, DEAR, I HAVE A HEADACHE

Sometimes you really do have a King Kong headache. Or you are just too tired or not in the mood or feeling put down or crotchety. Maybe he has "Friday night fever" but you don't. How do you turn him down?

Whatever the reason for your reluctance, there are nice ways to say no, positive ways that won't turn things sour and will leave the door open for good times ahead. One woman added a bit of humor by hanging a sign on the bedroom door: "Aspirin Night Tonight. Rain Check Available." Her husband had the privilege of helping himself from an envelope of official-looking rain checks attached to the knob. Other ideas:

- "There's nobody I'd rather have ask, but . . ."
- "We always have such a good time, but not tonight."
- "You're a terrific lover, but I'm suffering overload."
- "Let's make an appointment for Tuesday at nine instead."
- "What an offer! But I have to pass on this one for now."
- "I'm so glad you asked! . . . but . . ."
- "Can we have a drink and snack together instead? I need to catch up on my sleep."
- "Nobody does it better, but . . ."
- "I've had a hard day. I just want you to hold me instead."
- "You're the love of my life even on nights when I turn you down. I never stop loving you."
- "We'll make up for it next time."
- "Just because your Snow White has the flu and is sneezy and dopey tonight doesn't mean she'll be grumpy or sleepy or any of those other ghastly little gremlins next week."

- P.S. #1: In a day or two, post a big sign where your mate can see it: "My Headache Is Gone."
- P.S. #2: Don't let it bother you all that much if sex isn't so good once or twice. Why take it so seriously? Next time will be better, and the two of you have a lifetime ahead.

It's Just As Hard to Live with Someone You Love As It Is to Love Someone You Live With

Learning to overcome those unpleasant marriage encounters

There is no remedy for love but to love more.

HENRY DAVID THOREAU, *Journal*

Opposites attract. Opposites can also attack.

Morning people often marry night people. Each is bothered by the other's routine. Neatniks hook up with Sloppy Susies. Miss Society marries Mr. Social Misfit, so one can't wait for parties to begin while the other can't wait for them to end. You're planning for next year; he's enjoying today. Egos collide and personal styles grate. Welcome to the rest of your life!

Noted writer G. K. Chesterton said, "If Americans can be divorced for 'incompatibility,' I cannot conceive why they are not all divorced. I have known many happy marriages, but never a compatible one. The whole aim of marriage is to fight through and survive the instant when incompatibility becomes unquestionable. For a man and woman, as such, are incompatible." You can't have a relationship without tension, but counselor and author Sonya Rhodes says, "I always tell couples that 90 percent of the issues that they bicker about can probably be overlooked."

Happiness isn't always the absence of conflict, but rather knowing how to cope with the inevitable frustrations that come along. Out of the whirlpool of differing opinions can come deeper insights, mutual acceptance, and stronger ties that turn struggles into stepping stones. Disagreeing agreeably is really a labor of love, because it serves the healthy purpose of seeking a settlement. Relationships made strong by the resolution of conflicts endure. Learning to be open about and discuss things that bother us can make us more contented people. It is much, much more rewarding to solve a problem than to dissolve a partnership.

Maybe you or your partner are not at all sure that there can be a good marriage after arguing. Typically, those who feel this way have been brought up in households where children heard parents bicker all the time over small unimportant matters or whose moms and dads never faced the real underlying issues head-on because they believed anger is wrong and that open discussion of differing opinions would forever destroy a relationship. Understandably, conflict of any kind is so terrifying to people with this type of upbringing that they will do almost anything to sidestep every unpleasant issue. Just walking away or pretending everything is OK seems easier.

Running off and withdrawing from discussion can be done physically, by walking out of the room, or mentally, by not listening and responding appropriately, by changing the subject, avoiding eye contact, and withholding honest opinions, or making jokes. Done regularly, these patterns are extremely destructive. These partners do not understand that open and honest discussion, even if heated, is not the same as fighting. Rather, it is letting each other know what is in your mind and emotions when there is discord, and then trying for a solution. Partners who withdraw may eventually make up, but both will be walking on eggshells again next week when the same pattern resurfaces. Nothing ever gets solved, and some couples avoid conflict for a lifetime until after a while, *Mayday!* One or the other will probably want out, or they end up in a silent, resentful, and bitter old-age rage. If solid talk seems harsh to you, think of it as planning or discussion or laying the groundwork for good future relations. Take a peek at the test "Are You Afraid to Fight?" on page 174 to see if you are an avoider, someone who runs away from conflict.

If any of you lacks wisdom, let him ask of God, who gives to all men generously and without reproach, and it will be given to him.

JAMES 1:5, NASB

DO YOU CARE ENOUGH TO CONFRONT?

One couple calls their attempts to resolve conflicts "caring times," when they make an appointment with each other to talk things out. Here is their little cram course with a few simple ground rules to keep order when the showdowns come:

- We agree that disagreement is not evil.
- We will pick an appropriate time and place to talk as soon after the event as possible to avoid the building of resentment.
- We will not discuss emotional issues in front of the kids or just before bedtime or when one or the other is ready to walk out the door. We will delay talks until our minds are clear.
- We will work on one issue at a time.
- We will stay on the subject. No rabbit trails or past garbage from other arguments allowed.
- We will not scream or threaten or interrupt each other.
- No blaming. We will always be asking, "How can we solve this problem?" not "Why do we have this problem?" Our goal is to understand each other and find a solution, not to determine who is right or wrong.
- No fair either one taking our marbles and stalking off. That is what kids do.

Even when we are irritated, conflict
must be resolved.
- If we don't come to some agreement,
we will make a definite appointment
to talk again soon.

SOME OTHER HELPS AND HINTS TO KEEP
DISCUSSION SANE

❀ ❀ ❀

During discussion, learn the rhythm of talk,
then quiet. Talk, then more quiet. Long pauses
for introspection and consideration of the
other's point of view are essential. Constant
talk gives no time for reflection or for new
constructive thoughts to make headway.

It is best to listen much, speak little.

JAMES 1:19

❀ ❀ ❀

Know what you want and how you feel.
This does not come easily for those who
have always been people pleasers. Fear of
being unspiritual or selfish prompts some
folks to avoid looking at their own real
desires or expressing them openly. Those
who have always guarded their own hearts

146

by hiding feelings may not have asked themselves for decades, "What do I want? What are my feelings about this or that?"

Once you know exactly what you want, use simple words and a kind voice to let the other know. Be explicit and talk calmly to tell what is bothering you and why you feel as you do. Exaggerated statements like "Your mother hates everybody" are not acceptable. Complaining or whining will not generate enough empathy to get the message across. Just state the problem, and then suggest a reasonable change. What happens afterward is up to your partner. You have done your part. Sometimes it takes a long time for change to come about, so be patient. You are on your way.

Example: "I feel resentful when I see you go off each Saturday morning to enjoy a whole day of golf. I need help on weekends catching up on the week's housework. I would like it a lot if you could take over cleaning the den, bedroom, and bathrooms before you leave."

❀ ❀ ❀

Listen, then respond accordingly. Try to get behind the other's eyeballs to see things from his point of view. Read between the lines and ask yourself, "What is he *really* saying and feeling?" or "How would I feel in this situation?" If you still don't get it, ask aloud, "Tell me why you want that?" or "What are you feeling right now? Why?"

He who gives an answer before he hears, it is folly and shame to him.

PROVERBS 18:13, NASB

❀ ❀ ❀

You may sometimes think you need to provide a hearing aid to get your message across. One counselor asks couples to use an oven timer set for about three minutes, each committing to listen, *really* listen, to the other for that length of time without interrupting. After each speaks, the listener is asked to state the speaker's point of view aloud to be absolutely sure it is clearly understood.

❀ ❀ ❀

Know-it-alls get nowhere, so stay off your high horse! No fair demanding, threatening, preaching, or imploring. Stay away from expressions like "You must do . . ." or

"You should have done . . ." or "You had better do . . ." or "I expect you to . . ." Certain hostile voice inflections, facial expressions, and body postures can communicate distance or hate, too. Folded arms seem like a wall. Scowls and pointed fingers appear threatening. Sighs sometimes sound like self-pity. Is this any way to run a marriage?

❀ ❀ ❀

You *can't* be as nasty as you want to be! Couples know each other's flash points full well and how to hurt each other most. During the heat of argument, weak character spots are glaring. You can choose to claw at them with instant insults, or maneuver around them. It is nearly impossible to retract terrible words like "I never really loved you anyway" or "You never will amount to anything" or "You are fat and ugly" or "OK, go ahead and file for divorce; see if I care." The pain pounds away in the other's mind long after the rage that prompted the cruel words has ended.

Reckless words pierce like a sword, but the tongue of the wise brings healing.

PROVERBS 12:18

❑ From Elizabeth: "When we argue, I do not have to catch my man's mad mood nor copycat his ranting and raving by meeting his spells of rage with my own outbursts of anger. I have a choice. I may have the perfect put-downs in my mind, but I don't have to shout them aloud. Allowing him to trigger my rage only makes things worse. If I can keep my wits about me, I can sometimes choose to ignore the unpleasant things he says in his fit of madness and quietly walk away, saying, 'There will be a more appropriate time to talk about this later. Let's try again tomorrow.' Strangely, the issue often doesn't seem important the next day."

❀ ❀ ❀

Check yourself: Do you avoid eye contact, fidget, talk too fast or too loud, act uneasy by pacing back and forth during discussion, or let yourself be distracted by pets or the postman's arrival with mail? All of these tell the other that you would rather not be spending time talking through important issues and that you plan to leave the scene as soon as possible. Maybe this time you can sit down and stay the course without these adverse telltale gestures.

❀ ❀ ❀

As much as possible, use "I" messages, not "you," when talking together. The "I" pronoun simply reports how you see a situation and how you feel about it. It doesn't blame the other and is not judgmental.

Example:

- Best: "I felt hurt when you forgot to call from Cleveland like you promised. I felt worried about whether or not you arrived safely."
  Worst: "You hurt me and the kids by not calling. You made us all worry. Can't you ever get your act together when you travel?"
- Best: "I feel very angry right now."
  Worst: "You make me so mad!"
- Best: "I feel we need more time together."
  Worst: "You are gone too much! You need to take me out to dinner now and then."

❀ ❀ ❀

Good house rule: If one of you brings up a matter against the other, it is illegal to justify or deny it without literally pausing to consider that it may be true. Stubborn denial is frustrating to the other because it stonewalls a solution and takes away all hope for reconciliation. The only sensible approach is, "I'll think about that."

❀ ❀ ❀

If you are being wrongly accused, calmly say so and tell why. If not, admit the whole rotten truth about yourself and go on. Strong people make as many and as ghastly mistakes as weak people. The difference is that strong people admit them and learn from them.

If you refuse criticism, you will end in poverty and disgrace; if you accept criticism, you are on the road to fame.

PROVERBS 13:18, TLB

❀ ❀ ❀

If you are wrong, admit it. If right, shut up!

A man who refuses to admit his mistakes can never be successful. But if he confesses and forsakes them, he gets another chance.

PROVERBS 28:13, TLB

✿ ✿ ✿

If you apologize, be sure your apology is genuine and heartfelt and that a behavior change is planned. It is hollow indeed and will be perceived as lying if you say, "I'm sorry I have been late so often coming home for dinner," and then continue to hang out somewhere with friends night after night.

> ❏ From an army wife: "When I hear 'I'm sorry,' I also hear 'I love you.' When my husband and I sat at the kitchen table crying because of something awful he admitted, he knew it was time to apologize. It was all over for me when he said the wonderful words I needed to hear: 'I'm genuinely sorry. You have my word. I will not do that again, not ever. I see now how I have hurt you. If I ever slip, please let me know.'"

✿ ✿ ✿

Don't stop a heated discussion in a huff just because things get hot and uncomfortable. Conflict must be resolved. The issue must be settled. *The goal is not to think alike, but to think together.* Remember that the important middle stage in an argument is negotiation, when you listen to each other's views and begin to understand. Tempers are bound to flare more easily at this stage. Expect it and hang in there. Many couples never reach the satisfying resolution stage that comes along right afterward.

> ❑ From Jo: "If the hour is late and opinions are stalemated, but further talks are needed, we make an appointment for tomorrow. We let each other know that we are committed to our relationship, kiss good-night whether we feel like it or not (we usually don't), and rest peacefully."

❊ ❊ ❊

When deadlock comes, think of options. Say aloud, "We're the kind of people who can do better than this." Then generate as many possible solutions as you can. Write them down, even the far-fetched ones. None is to be ridiculed or ruled out, no matter how crazy or impractical or expensive. Arrange them in order of possible effectiveness, then each selects one idea to be tried for a day or a week, with reevaluation promised then. You may not accept the other's solution, but being willing to test the waters goes a long way toward creating trust and respect. If things aren't working out, try another idea. Then another. Keep at it.

❀ ❀ ❀

Solutions sometimes take generous amounts of compromise from both parties.
  Example:

- "I'll cut up my credit card if you will agree to set aside fifty dollars in personal spending money for me every week from our household budget."
- "Since you don't sleep well when you eat hearty at night, let's eat lighter on weeknights, then plan bigger evening meals like I prefer on Saturdays and Sundays."

▫ The same old argument about whether to have a fourth baby came up over and over again and got us nowhere. "No more children," my husband said firmly. With three girls,

I wanted to try for a boy. So I suggested that we each dump our frustrations and our mad feelings and make a list of the pros and cons of this dilemma on paper.

At first we felt awkward. The idea was so new. But, when we read through our lists together, the whys and wherefores became a lot clearer and we shared feelings calmly. No, we didn't make the decision right then, but we felt a lot closer to it, and when baby talk came up after that, we didn't just stalk away and pout. It was a start.

❀ ❀ ❀

When things get overheated during an argument, here are things to say that will let the other know you are still a team despite differences:

- "We are two good people who deserve a solution. We'll find one."
- "I am listening especially closely to you today. I want to understand how you feel."
- "We may not always get along, but

we both deserve a hearing, so let's get on with this discussion."

- "It does something good for our marriage when we can count on each other to stick around and hammer out differences instead of walking away."

❀ ❀ ❀

One of the best ways to stop the grinding, sniping pattern that couples often fall into is to remove the resistance. If you can purposefully find some part of your partner's statements that you agree with and say so, the other will likely run out of steam.

❀ ❀ ❀

Learn to walk the path less traveled. Now and then, stop the discussion long enough to pat yourselves on the back. You may not agree on everything, but perhaps you can say something positive like:

- "We sure have improved in the way we try to thrash out our problems. Remember when we couldn't talk at all about differences?"

- "I'm glad we agree that my mother can come to stay for a while. We've done a good job solving that issue. Now, all that is left to work on is how long she can be here."

❀ ❀ ❀

Things to say to yourself when things seem to get out of hand, the discussion is going nowhere, and your mind-set turns into frustration and anger:

- "It is not necessary for me to be right all the time."
- "Giving in is not a weakness."
- "Men and women see things differently. It's OK for us to have different views. It's not the end of the world."
- "Whatever my partner feels is right, let him express it. He has his reasons."
- "Be humble, thinking of others as better than yourself. Don't just think about your own affairs, but be interested in others, too, and in what they are doing [and saying]." Philippians 2:3-4, TLB

❀ ❀ ❀

Things *not* to say:

- "I can't help it if I'm the way I am.
  My whole family was always that
  way." No hand-me-down genes are
  allowed when it comes to relationships. Usually these patterns are
  learned from parents. Learned tactics
  can be unlearned.
- "You shouldn't feel that way." You
  can't control the other's feelings. He
  does feel that way. Try to find out
  why.
- "I can't be watching my words all the
  time." Yes, you really can! Uninten-
  tional words can hurt just as much!

❀ ❀ ❀

If an argument gets too hot to handle,
maybe you could ask to stop and pray
together. Some helpful prayers:

- "Lord, grant that I may seek more to
  understand than to be understood."
  (St. Francis of Assisi)
- "Lord, make us reasonable and kind
  as we deal with each other. Keep us
  from stubborn and unkind silences

and help us to understand the feelings and needs of the other. Put your words in our mouths to get this discussion done."

- "Lord, bring some good out of the events that brought on our argument. Teach us both how to live and love better because of this conflict."

TERRIFIC TACTICS FROM LONGTIME MARRIEDS

❀ ❀ ❀

When Norm and I are in the middle of a muddle, battling with each other, when the discussion is going nowhere and we begin to hurt each other with loud words, one of us calls, "Time Out!" We stop all talk and agree to go our separate ways. Usually he flops on the couch in the den and I take a brisk stroll around the block to calm down. We both understand that our short break isn't the same as walking out, and when we return in a few minutes, we are a lot less emotional, a lot more logical.

❀ ❀ ❀

From Alice: "Long ago, a wise pastor challenged me to write down a long, long list of my husband's good qualities. I keep it in the dresser drawer. On a day when I can't get over feeling resentful, I read over the entire list, one by one. In the midst of harsh words, the things I do admire about my husband often go unnoticed—his integrity, honesty, dependability, love of God, and faithfulness to family."

So then let us pursue the things which make for peace and the building up of one another.

ROMANS 14:19, NASB

Bonus idea: On a good day, maybe after making up, write all those good reasons you chose your partner on one of the kids' little blackboards or tack your list to the bulletin board in his workroom so he knows how you feel.

❀ ❀ ❀

Him? In God's image? When I consciously look for Christlike qualities in my mate and can truly perceive them, I never think of him as quite the same person again. It is honestly overwhelming to realize afresh that a holy spirit, a righteous spirit, an "I really would rather do right" spirit, a spirit of love, God's spirit, actually lives inside this man, even though, at the moment, we are arguing. He is made in God's image, too. He would really rather be loving me right now, too. Very simply, we are a good couple, two of God's beloved children, in the middle of a tough problem that needs solving.

❀ ❀ ❀

From marriage counselor Dennis Rainey: "If you want to practice loving confrontation, you can't believe your mate is out to get you, and you can't be out to get your mate. Be willing to hear what God may be saying through your mate. It could be that he is trying to send an important message to you through your partner. Some of us don't want to hear because we would rather be comfortable than Christlike. Many of my wife, Barbara's, best statements to me are the ones that hurt a bit, but I need to hear them."

❀ ❀ ❀

When I get really angry and want to lash out at my guy, I go by myself and sing a quieting hymn:

Drop Thy still dews of quietness,
Till all our strivings cease;
Take from our souls the strain and stress,
And let our ordered lives confess
The beauty of Thy peace.

JOHN GREENLEAF WHITTIER

WHAT IS FORGIVENESS?

❀ ❀ ❀

Forgiveness means giving up your rights to hang on to a grudge or to punish the other, even though you have been wronged. It means attempting to forget as quickly as you can.

It is not our capacity to think that makes us
different from animals, but our capacity to repent
and to forgive. Only humans can perform that
most unnatural act, and by doing so they can
develop relationships that transcend
the relentless law of nature.

A. SOLZHENITSYN

He who forgives first, wins.

WILLIAM PENN

To forgive is to set a prisoner free . . . and discover
that the prisoner was you.

DR. LEWIS SMEDES

163

◻ From a Georgia wife of forty years: "I try to remember to pray for my husband if I feel I have been wronged. I do it while I am still angry (often very, very difficult), but I go ahead anyway, just because Jesus said!

"We human beings pray for new cars, health, more money, and a thousand other tangible things, so why isn't it reasonable to pray good character qualities into my mate, things like more sensitivity to my needs and the children's, the ability to listen or to admit mistakes, more openness to others' opinions and ideas, the ability to confront me with kindness when things go wrong? I have found that God answers a large percentage of these kinds of prayers! Yet I rarely hear anybody talking about praying for troublesome companions."

Love your enemies, do good to those who hate you, bless those who curse you, pray for those who mistreat you.
LUKE 6:27-28

◻ One husband reported to marriage counselor Dr. Cecil Osborne: My wife and I had reached an impasse. The occasional times we talked to each other, there were cold, impersonal comments, often critical ones. "Look, I have a suggestion," I said. "For the next three months, let's have an amicable separation, a kind of psychic divorce, but continue living together. During this time, let's agree that there are to be no complaints or criticisms from either one of us." She agreed.

My wife began being nicer to me, and I automatically started to respond a bit. I began to be more helpful around the house, and she reacted by being somewhat more affectionate. I started to pay compliments more often. She became more loving, and from then on it's been good. We rarely criticize or complain; there's little or nothing to complain about. We just tried hard to meet each other's needs and it worked miracles.

❀ ❀ ❀

When the going gets rough and the two of you feel swamped with resentment and overcome with anger, remember the bright side of disagreement: Even a seed has to be buried before it can produce a good crop. Can you use every relationship problem to produce a positive effect? Will it get you to a counselor? Is it helping you see the personal problems behind the symptoms? Can you say someday, "If this had never happened, we'd still be in our misery, with no hope"?

HOW TO MAKE MAKING UP FUN (WITH A LITTLE INTENSIVE CARING AND SOME FORETHOUGHT)

❀ ❀ ❀

Even acts of contrition can be fun. Stick up appropriate Post-it notes with your heartfelt words, or have your message painted on a new T-shirt. Better yet, write it on a slip of paper to be secretly sneaked into his wallet or between the pages of a book he is reading:

- I'm sorry! I feel like the Queen of Mean.
- *Chomp, chomp.* That's the sound of me eating my words.
- I would marry you all over again.
- Mary loves Jerry today, too.

- We belong together even if we argue sometimes.
- We've been silly and outrageous. Let's make up.
- It's you and me, Babe.
- I care about us.

☐ Once when we were mad at each other, I went into the den where he was hiding behind the evening newspaper and blinked the flashlight on and off at him, over and over. Puzzled and still annoyed, he asked, "What do you think you are doing?" The sunshine came back into his eyes when I said, "I'm telling you in Morse code that I love you anyway and want to make up."

❀ ❀ ❀

Cut out funny cartoons or comics that spoof your situation, or piece together humorous phrases from newspaper headlines or words from magazine ads. Tape them all over—on his telephone, computer screen, car steering wheel, and exercise bike.

☐ We went to bed angry because there was a terrible gulf of misunderstanding after a bad argument. I called my husband the next morning at the office and told him I had been thinking about yesterday's argument. "I hated the bad words, yelling, and screaming," I said, "but I think we are learning a lot about how (and how not) to tell our feelings to each other. I like that. Hollering doesn't work. We'll do better next time." He told me later that he felt better because I called, that it connected us again.

❀ ❀ ❀

After tempers cool, agree that each of you will write down the other's three most troublesome habits to be posted on the refrigerator door. Every time one of you is caught doing one of these annoying things, the other will get an advantage like a five-dollar cash penalty fee paid from the offender's pocket, a fifty-point advantage in the next rummy game, or a handicap advantage in golf. It's a friendly way to keep reminding each other that change is expected.

A wife is to thank God that her husband
has faults; a husband without faults
is a dangerous observer.

LORD HALIFAX

❀ ❀ ❀

String a big banner that says MAKING
UP IS FUN TO DO, SO LET'S! across
the living room when he comes home from
work.

❀ ❀ ❀

Write a true-to-life short story or poem
based on the two of you, your happiness,
and your problems. Add stick-figure
sketches showing the lead characters
sometimes loving, sometimes arguing. Be
sure they romance each other at the end
and live happily ever after. Attach a
cover and leave your literary masterpiece sitting next to his morning coffeepot or mail it to his office marked
"Personal."

❀ ❀ ❀

Make the most of the kid inside each of
you to help get a laugh out of your frustrations, fears, and foibles. Write your

making-up message on the "world's larg-est" inflated balloon so it poofs out of its hiding place when he opens the closet door. For extra fun, load up his small bathroom or hobby room with a couple of dozen balloons with marvelous messages written all over.

□ After a nasty argument, one wife placed her small son's toy sailboat on her husband's desk with the striking message: "The best thing we can do for our marriage is to get out!" In smaller letters: "Let's get away to get some sun, sand, beach, and a tan where it doesn't show. Good talk comes better there."

❀ ❀ ❀

Have appropriate Bible passages marked, then ask if the two of you (peeved though you may be) can read the selected Scriptures together. One wife calls it "chicken soup for our attitudes."

Forgiving each other, just as God in Christ also has forgiven you.

EPHESIANS 4:32, NASB

*Above all, keep fervent in your love for one
another, because love covers a multitude of sins.*

1 PETER 4:8, NASB

*Now we who are strong ought to bear the
weaknesses of those without strength and not* just
please ourselves.

ROMANS 15:1, NASB

*Love is very patient and kind, never jealous or
envious, never boastful or proud, never haughty
or selfish or rude. Love does not demand its own
way. It is not irritable or touchy. It does not hold
grudges and will hardly even notice when others
do it wrong. It is never glad about injustice, but
rejoices whenever truth wins out. If you love
someone you will be loyal to him, no matter what
the cost. You will always believe in him, always
expect the best of him, and always stand your
ground in defending him.*

1 CORINTHIANS 13:4-7, TLB

*Never act from motives of rivalry or personal
vanity, but in humility think more of each other
than you do of yourselves. None of you should
think only of his own affairs, but consider other
people's interests also.*

PHILIPPIANS 2:3-4, Phillips

Do to others what you would have them do to you.

Don't just pretend that you love others: really love them. Hate what is wrong. Stand on the side of the good. Love each other with brotherly affection and take delight in honoring each other.

ROMANS 12:9-10, TLB

Let all bitterness and wrath and anger and clamor and slander be put away from you, along with all malice. And be kind to one another, tender-hearted, forgiving each other, just as God in Christ also has forgiven you.

EPHESIANS 4:31-32, NASB

Be humble and gentle. Be patient with each other, making allowance for each other's faults because of your love.

EPHESIANS 4:2, TLB

Your attitude should be the kind that was shown us by Jesus . . . who did not demand and cling to his rights.

PHILIPPIANS 2:5-6, TLB

❀ ❀ ❀

Maybe you feel like you need to bring
your therapist home to help handle discord

172

at your house. The cheaper way is to take advantage of one of the many great marriage enrichment seminars offered by churches and counseling centers and wonderful books written to teach couples the how-tos of a good relationship. Invite your mate to read some of these with you. Reading aloud in front of the fireplace on a cold night can bring a nice feeling of oneness.

P.S. You will each spend seven years of your life in the bathroom. Maybe you will need a good book.

Caring Enough to Confront by David Augsburger (Herald Press, 1980)

Love for a Lifetime by Dr. James Dobson (Word, 1995)

I Love You, But Why Are We So Different? by Tim LaHaye (Harvest House Publishers, 1991)

When Anger Hits Home: Taking Care of Your Anger Without Taking It Out on Your Family by H. Norman Wright (Moody Press, 1992)

Choosing to Love Again by Gary Rosberg (Focus on the Family Publishing, 1992)

Angry Book by Dr. Theodore I. Rubin (Macmillan, 1970)

When You Don't Agree by James Fairfield
(Herald Press, 1977)
Courtship after Marriage by Zig Ziglar
(Ballantine Books, 1992)

ARE YOU AFRAID TO FIGHT?

Avoiders will tell you that they only want
peace. But counselors almost always agree
that refusing to discuss important issues,
especially in marriage, has exactly the
opposite effect, heightening the conflict as
well as the partner's anger and resentment.
Stubborn avoidance seems cowardly,
besides.

If you answer yes to several of the questions below, you are probably somebody
who is inclined to walk away from problems rather than to stay and face them
with your mate. Will your partner who
comes to you hoping for good talk and a
compromise or solution simply walk away
from you in hopeless frustration? Think
about it.

1. Do you feel it is wrong to disagree
   or get angry?
2. Are you caught in the "Everything is
   OK" syndrome, even when your feel-

ings tell you different or your mate brings up a troublesome problem? Avoiders often refuse to admit there is anything wrong so tough situations never have to be addressed.

3. Has it been a long time since you discussed things like money or sex or in-laws eyeball-to-eyeball with your mate?

4. Do you often make excuses when your partner asks to talk together about important issues? Do you have difficulty finding just the right time or place? Are you always afraid the children or neighbors will hear, or would you likely excuse yourself because the Golf World Classic is on television?

5. Are there one or two dangerous subjects to be avoided because they always bring shouting or tears?

6. Would you rather buy a gift for your partner to try to soothe resentments than deal with the problem by talking? Counselors say this is a favorite ploy of husbands.

7. When conflict begins, do you often give in quickly "before someone's

feelings are hurt" rather than stand up for your point of view?

8. Has it been more than six months since you challenged your mate with something like "What's eating you lately?" or by bringing up an issue of your own with words like "There is something bothering me; let's talk."

The Twin Marriage Slayers
Breaking the boredom cycle
when the cash flow is low

True Love is but a humble, low-born thing,
And hath its food served up in earthen ware;
It is a thing to walk with, hand in hand,
through the everydayness of this workday world.

JAMES RUSSELL LOWELL, *Love*

Maybe you have a sinking feeling that something is wrong, but you're not sure what. You don't look forward to good times on weekends with your spouse anymore, and it's harder to find things to talk and laugh about when you go to restaurants. It's not the occasional two or three days of sluggish monotony that spell trouble. Everybody gets afflicted with the winter blahs or summer slump or bogged down now and then during hard times. It's the day in, day out "same stuff," lived over and over again, without enthusiasm, nothing new added, that kills closeness. Now really, how many reruns can you watch?

"We've gone through two refrigerator light bulbs in six months trying to fill the void between us," says one wife. "We're good people, but we just don't seem to know how to be a couple anymore. We're dry as dust."

There are no five-minute miracles promised here. But a daily or weekly dose of something new might pull a yawning relationship out of recession and bring back that warm and satisfying feeling of connectedness. Nearness and dearness grow best with time spent enjoying each other in fresh ways.

How to break free of boredom when your checkbook is teetering on the edge of being overdrawn? Create some fun from nothing (or next to it) with these terrific stay-at-home ideas, but be sure the activity you choose is something you both will enjoy.

❀ ❀ ❀

Armchair travel mating: Collect brochures ahead of time and plan a summer vacation while you munch on pizza or popcorn balls.

❀ ❀ ❀

Choose a country; choose a video. Then settle into your deepest sofa for armchair travel to obscure places until you feel like you're falling off the map. Visit remote palm-lined beaches. Choose the countries you'll visit when you win the ten-million-dollar sweepstakes that Ed McMahon is always talking about. Pay a call to a different place each night for a week.

❀ ❀ ❀

Popcorn theater for two: Rent two or three flicks for one sitting, then cuddle up to a romantic or sentimental evening at home. Bored with the latest from Hollywood? Choose a classic, a musical, a stand-up comic, or try something with subtitles.

❀ ❀ ❀

Pull off an entertainment bargain by blatantly planning a television evening at home. Supply snacks and drinks and check off in the *TV Guide* with bright-red pencil what the two of you would most likely enjoy. Or "toon in" on cable to Bugs Bunny and Donald Duck and laugh like when you were kids.

❀ ❀ ❀

Choose from a thousand topics a new
hobby to learn together via video. Study
Spanish, bootstrap investing, furniture
refinishing, carving, or how to make
money by buying up real estate.

❀ ❀ ❀

Any night can be dance night at your
house. There is no cover charge in this private club, and you get to choose the tunes.
Roll up the rugs to rock 'n' roll your way
through the living room and kitchen with
Elvis or fox-trot cheek to cheek listening
to a Glenn Miller tape. Don't know how to
dance? Rent a how-to video for the cha-
cha or rumba or West Coast swing.

❀ ❀ ❀

Organize family photos in groups and
mount them in an album as a gift to your
parents, your children, or yourselves.
Rehash old times while sorting.

❀ ❀ ❀

Make up family trees for your children or
begin a written family history. Fortunately,
this project takes two for best results.

✽ ✽ ✽

Sit together and address Christmas cards
or write thank-you notes for gifts received.
Or spend an hour writing notes of encouragement to church folks who have been ill
or discouraged.

✽ ✽ ✽

Figure out which holiday traditions you
want for your family. Opening Christmas
gifts the night before? New Year's at the
beach? Cornucopias and roast beef at
Thanksgiving "just because"? Bright idea:
One family places three kernels of dried
corn and a tiny basket at each place
around the Thanksgiving table. One at a
time, before the food is passed, each person puts the corn kernels inside their basket, telling the three things for which they
are most thankful. For other ideas to make
holiday traditions more meaningful: *Great
Christmas Ideas* by Alice Chapin (Tyndale
House, 1992).

✽ ✽ ✽

Make yours a working marriage. Pick up a
bucket and brush to clean up the car or
wash all eighteen windows in your house.

Become willing dust busters and clean up the place top to bottom. Even if it means getting grungy, enjoy trying out the latest in cleaning products. Do you experience junk overload? Come to order by purging every closet and the garage of unwanted items. Kiss kitchen clutter good-bye by getting cupboards organized. Nice work! Now is the time to make some money selling all those things you forgot you had.

❀ ❀ ❀

Swap chores. Whatever "him" and "her" jobs have been established in your home, turn them around. Each of you will better appreciate all that the other does around home. Maybe you could swap male-female roles in romancing each other, too. Think about it.

❀ ❀ ❀

Cook gourmet together for an afternoon. See *Romantic Meals for Lovers: Recipes for 50 Intimate Occasions* by Gabrielle Kirschbaum (Prima, 1987).

❀ ❀ ❀

Be creative with routine stuff. One couple found themselves arguing over who would

walk the dog each morning before they
rushed off to work. Both realized how
little time they had to spend together, so
they agreed to get up a little earlier and
join forces to take Jasper for his morning
stroll. Now they look forward to their
walks and are exploring parts of the neighborhood they never would see otherwise
(Jasper, too!). Both agree that their morning freshness often helps them walk and
talk their way through problems and ideas
better than when they wait until night,
when both are weary from work.

❀ ❀ ❀

Stay home and wash or color each other's
hair.

❀ ❀ ❀

Read to each other. Go through an
armload of joke books or humor columns
in the newspaper. Choose a mystery that
will curl your hair. Check out a how-to
book that interests both of you. What
about reading through the Bible in a year?
Write the American Bible Society for a
suggested schedule at P.O. Box 5656,
Grand Central Station, New York,

NY 10164-0851. Or maybe each of you could read an interesting book separately and then get together to kick around the ideas and share opinions. Some say that this is the way big decisions for change come about. See the resource list at the end of this book.

❀ ❀ ❀

Quiet hours spent reading together in the library are nice, too. Check out the superb selection of fascinating new magazines you cannot afford to have sent to your home.

❀ ❀ ❀

Get the morning shower-and-breakfast routine out of the way and take on the new habit of reading together each day from an inspirational book like *Daily Guideposts* from Guideposts, Carmel, NY 10512 or *Quiet Times for Couples* by H. Norman Wright (Harvest House, 1990).

❀ ❀ ❀

How long since you've enjoyed a Sunday evening of fun and games like rummy, chess, Monopoly, or Chinese checkers? Plan a week-long tournament and keep

score on a wall chart. Winner takes all the
contents of the penny jar you've been
using as a doorstop. Or just be spontaneous and toss around a Frisbee or don baseball mitts for a game of catch. Refresh
your memory on being silly: Remember
how the two of you used to poke and joke
and chase each other when you first dated?

❀ ❀ ❀

Put together Wal-Mart's biggest jigsaw
puzzle—5,000 pieces! You assemble one
part, he the other. Have you seen the mystery puzzles where you read the booklet,
then become the detective as you piece
together the hidden clues? There's nothing
quite like the intrigue of a whodunit.

❀ ❀ ❀

Gather a basketful of catalogs—sports,
clothing, collector's items, gifts, jewelry,
whatever interests you both. Go through
them together with a marking pen to plan
your dream bedroom or select the best
appliances for your remodeled kitchen.
Catalog stores are never crowded, and you
can do your Christmas shopping twenty-
four hours a day wearing comfortable pj's.

❀ ❀ ❀

Enter contests together. Two heads are better
than one to think up slogans and limericks.
Two sets of hands make addressing envelopes
and writing out name, address, and zip code
on three-by-five cards faster. Subscribe to a
contest magazine so you don't miss deadlines
and to find those with the best prizes. Bring
home entry blanks from grocery and drug
stores. You'd like to win a trip to Cancun or
ten thousand dollars, wouldn't you?

❀ ❀ ❀

Bring home lollipops, sticks, and penny
candy or ingredients for root-beer floats,
candied apples, or ice-cream sundaes to
enjoy while watching the hummingbird
wars around the backyard feeder.

❀ ❀ ❀

On a hot summer day, dump a few bags of
ice into the backyard pool to cool things
off. Raid the children's toy chest for water
pistols and beach balls.

❀ ❀ ❀

It's winter now. Throw on a heavy coat,
hat, muffler, gloves, and boots to take a

walk in the park right after a snowstorm.
Go tobogganing or sledding, make paths
through pristine places, and spread-eagle
on the ground to make snow angels. Toss a
blanket and lay out a picnic. Build a snow-
man and an impenetrable white fort, then
have a snowball battle. Bet you can enlist a
few kids for this one.

❀ ❀ ❀

Get growing! Plant a garden. You plant
flowers, he plants vegetables. Look for
exotic seeds, or stick with the tried-and-
true tomato or pepper plants. Your home
horticulture will pay off in a few weeks
when you make chili or spaghetti sauce
together.

❀ ❀ ❀

Take an arm-in-arm walk in the moonlight
or share an umbrella in the rain. Talk
about your future together. Reminisce
about your love affair. Go home and read
aloud old love letters to each other.

❀ ❀ ❀

Have your own private marriage enrichment weekend at home. Jeans and tees are

in order, and there's no need for him to shave off that sensual stubble. Rent a Homebuilders videotape from Family Life Conferences, P.O. Box 23840, Little Rock, AR 72221. Write in workbook answers as you talk them through together. Have pizza sent in.

❀ ❀ ❀

Remember that bowl of leftover cookie dough you stashed away in the freezer just before Christmas? It's time now to get it out and bake up a batch with your beloved. Serve your incredible edibles fresh from the oven with hot chocolate and top it all with whipped cream.

❀ ❀ ❀

Take a vacation from your diet to make candied apples or fudge.

❀ ❀ ❀

Perhaps he's raved over Aunt Cary's molasses cookies or his mom's German potato salad for years. Now is the time to try out some favorite recipes. One couple enjoyed making root beer right in their own kitchen. Maybe the two of you could prepare a big dinner. You do the main course. He bakes up the chocolate cheesecake. What about decorating America's funniest home pizzas for two? Welcome any and all unexpected culinary catastrophes with laughter.

❀ ❀ ❀

Cook a goose for Christmas dinner to take to his mother's house. You'll love raving about the fun you had doing it together, and you can gloat over your succulent success in front of everybody. Perhaps you two could join free cooking school classes, then invite holiday guests to reap the results with you. Or buy a new wok and create a stir at dinner.

❀ ❀ ❀

Bake a beautiful unbirthday cake for a friend. Frost it, crank up a couple of quarts of homemade ice cream, then deliver it all.

❀ ❀ ❀

Carve a jack-o'-lantern.

❀ ❀ ❀

So your idea of something to do is nothing to do. Then purposefully wipe your Saturday slate clean and plan nothing at all. Whatever will busy folks like you end up doing? Anything at all, as long as it isn't something you have to do! Putter. Linger over breakfast coffee. Walk around the yard to check on flowers you planted. Tidy up your desk. Hey! Just let it happen.

❀ ❀ ❀

The weather outside may be frightful, but you can warm up your winter by planning an indoor picnic with some hot eats by the fireplace. Roast hot dogs, chestnuts, or marshmallows, then talk to your heart's content.

Got a little wampum in your wallet, but not much? Need togetherness? Shazam! This continuing list of date-your-mate ideas that cost next to nothing just might be the magic ingredient to help you two go places again without spending away this month's mortgage payment. Best bets for getting the good times rolling on a bare-bones budget:

❀ ❀ ❀

Go on a most-for-your-money spree in the mall. Allow yourselves fifty cents or five dollars. Show off your fantastic finds when you get home and decide who got the most loot for money spent. Take advantage of blue-light specials in stores.

❀ ❀ ❀

Go grocery shopping with frugal "pantry fortification" as your aim. Stock your shelves with various items you find on great sales all over town.

❀ ❀ ❀

Buy or rent a video about middle management (how to trim the waist and tummy), then exercise together to whittle off some weight. Look for free newspaper coupons offering tryouts on exciting exercise equipment at the local spa. Enjoy it? Maybe your purse will allow joining for one month only.

❀ ❀ ❀

Find a bench in the middle of the mall or park your car on Main Street if you live in a small town and catch up on people watching. Maybe you could afford a triple-scoop ice-cream cone.

❀ ❀ ❀

You have been saving all year, so now you have Christmas money. Invite him to go holiday shopping with you.

❀ ❀ ❀

Take the downtown bus to go window shopping just to see what's new or silly or sensational. Fantasize your way through dazzling displays in the most expensive departments—jewelry, furniture, china. Try out new cosmetics and sample perfumes. Pick out designer clothes, fancy underwear, and expensive eye shades to look chic in the sun.

❀ ❀ ❀

For a little gas money, you can visit specialty stores to look for things that involve a particular hobby like boating, or skiing, or baseball cards, or whatever else you love. You'll know how to spend cash next time you have it. Look in the yellow pages to find:

- Pawn shops
- Farmer's markets
- Army-Navy supply stores
- Secondhand stores and thrift shops

- Specialty bookstores
- An incredible big-city superstore with everything from cantaloupes to computers
- Greeting card shops
- Fancy department stores
- Airport or hotel gift shops
- Fancy home-building supply places
- An old country store

❀ ❀ ❀

Attend grand openings for new grocery stores, gas stations, or other shops to register for valuable giveaways.

❀ ❀ ❀

Be on hand for big events in a nearby big city. Enjoy the excitement of crowds gathered for the first game of the World Series, the grand opening of the Big Dome, New Year's in Underground Atlanta or Times Square, Fourth of July fireworks at the mall, or other happenings like the July parade of yachts in West Palm Beach.

❀ ❀ ❀

Ever been to an auction? Sometimes there are incredible surprises when auctioneers pile dozens of items in a box to be sold as a unit. Even *you* can afford to make a dollar bid.

❊ ❊ ❊

Go garage sale-ing. Look in the classified section of the paper for just about any kind imaginable.

❊ ❊ ❊

Visit a thrift shop to search out neat repeats in clothing for you and the kids.

❊ ❊ ❊

Tour model homes. Choose your dream house and get ideas for redecorating.

❊ ❊ ❊

Browse out-of-the way shops for antiques and country uniques.

❊ ❊ ❊

Find a band concert in the park. Go early to roast weenies and marshmallows. Try to locate glowing charcoals left by previous picnickers.

❊ ❊ ❊

Attend a pet show. Ooh and aah over massive Percheron horses, a wrinkled and lovable Georgia bulldog, or a snooty pug-nosed blue-gray Persian kitty. You'll see exquisite animals you never knew existed.

❀ ❀ ❀

Meet your mate anywhere that's different, at a health-food store or restaurant, at a big-city museum snack bar, or maybe at a particular park bench with two brown bag lunches in hand and corn for the pigeons and squirrels. How about taking off work for a Thursday dollar-movie matinee?

❀ ❀ ❀

Head out at midnight for a sandwich at an all-night restaurant.

❀ ❀ ❀

Go fast-food restaurant hopping; then visit an interesting pet shop.

❀ ❀ ❀

Tour a local cannery or candy factory.

❀ ❀ ❀

Browse a big bookstore for a couple of hours.

❀ ❀ ❀

Watch for a dress rehearsal of a local concert or little theater play and just sit in. Many performers would welcome a good-looking audience of two, just like you.

❀ ❀ ❀

Watch a local professional sports team work out. No cost here to see the "pros" up close.

❀ ❀ ❀

On a hot August evening, visit a local indoor ice rink. Glide away gracefully, twirling and whirling while the inside temperature stays sane. Or play hookey for an afternoon and meet inside a local video arcade.

❀ ❀ ❀

Wheel and deal, sort of. Test drive new cars. A Caddy? A Porsche? A VW convertible? Your mind will already be made up when your jalopy runs no more.

❀ ❀ ❀

Go vote together. Talk about it ahead all week. Be the only ones on the block who make a big affair of it. Go out for coffee and doughnuts afterward and watch election results together at night. Maybe your candidate will make an exciting comeback.

❀ ❀ ❀

Go to a parade—Memorial Day, Veterans Day, St. Patrick's Day, Boy Scouts, a local pet parade. Get in the spirit of things by waving flags wildly and hooting and hollering when your favorite band passes by. On a cold day, get something hot brewing in the coffeepot afterward.

❀ ❀ ❀

Get wet. Borrow equipment to go bodysurfing, snorkeling, waterskiing, sailing, canoeing, or fishing. Go swimming and smooch underwater.

❀ ❀ ❀

Attend Little (or Big) League baseball games.

❀ ❀ ❀

Get a new hobby like orienteering, which will teach you to navigate along unfamiliar terrain. No costly equipment needed except a compass. The objective is to find all the control points and complete the course in the shortest time. A great sport for even the directionally impaired! Look in the community activities section of your newspaper to join local orienteering groups.

❀ ❀ ❀

Lose track of time by walking together on a beach somewhere. Hold hands while you stroll in the sand. Let the gentle surf cool your toes. Idle chitchat not forbidden. You packed cold chicken and a thermos of lemonade, didn't you?

❀ ❀ ❀

Visit a local garden spot or state or county park. Swing on swings or hike trails and identify flora and fauna. Search for four-leaf clovers. Skip rocks on the lake.

❀ ❀ ❀

Hoof it. Take a walk together in the neighborhood, maybe under the street lights or in the rain. Carve your initials on a tree in your own yard and play around with the neighbor's dog. Daydream about buying houses for sale.

Get wet. Borrow equipment to go bodysurfing, snorkeling, water skiing, sailing, canoeing, or fishing. Go swimming and smooch underwater.

❀ ❀ ❀

Take a ride out in the country or into
nearby mountains with no particular destination in mind. Collect autumn leaves for
pressing. Get lost.

❀ ❀ ❀

Pick your own fruit in an orchard; then
take it home to make jam.

❀ ❀ ❀

Get a guidebook and brochures from the
local chamber of commerce and visit cor-
ners of your little world you didn't know
existed. There are lots of statues of famous
heroes and roadside plaques to be investi-
gated, as well as historical houses and
memorial parks.

❀ ❀ ❀

Donate blood at the local blood bank.

❀ ❀ ❀

Mark "Mystery Destination" on both your
calendars for 6:30 P.M. on Friday. You'll be
driving, so keep your companion guessing
by taking scenic back roads through the
countryside, maybe to a famous barbecue

On a hot summer day, dump a few bags
of ice into the backyard pool to cool things off.
Raid the children's toy chest for
water pistols and beach balls.

spot or a brand-new yogurt place, where two-for-one sundaes are offered. Could you plan a ride each month for a while just to keep the fun going? Visit a long-lost college chum who just moved back to town or drop in to see exhibits at a planetarium or art gallery.

❀ ❀ ❀

Drive the historic homes tour in your city.

❀ ❀ ❀

Visit distant cousins you haven't seen in years, an elderly relative in a nursing home, an aged uncle who lives alone. Stay and bake him a pie.

❀ ❀ ❀

Visit a parish cemetery and identify well-known graves or those of long-gone relatives. Snap pictures, write down some sentimental or humorous sayings you find on tombstones, or make rubbings of interesting engravings.

❀ ❀ ❀

Visit a cattle, horse, or hog farm. Empty out the penny jar and "pig out" at a local barbecue place afterward.

❀ ❀ ❀

Next Sunday is Super Sunday. You two
have made up your minds to begin going
to church once again like you knew you
should all along! You will be there early
enough for Sunday school; then stay for
coffee and get acquainted.

Alternate idea: If you already attend regularly, go to church by radio some Sunday
morning just for a change of pace. Or be
on hand for Sunday evening services you
don't usually attend.

❀ ❀ ❀

Experience some holy nights at Christmas
by attending midnight mass or watchnight
or other special services at church.

❀ ❀ ❀

Look in the newspaper for free local
church choir or orchestra concerts or helpful seminars and support groups sponsored
by various denominations.

❀ ❀ ❀

Volunteer to serve together on the church
hall decorating committee, do nursery duty
as a team once a month, or help out at the

downtown soup kitchen when it is your church's turn to provide people.

IF YOU HAPPEN TO HAVE A BIT OF CASH—

❀ ❀ ❀

Rent a tandem bike. Turn some heads by renting some stunning turn-of-the-century clothes from a local theatrical costume store.

❀ ❀ ❀

Away you go to the country music festival! There'll be plenty of pickin' and pluckin' and drummin' and grinnin' somewhere near you this weekend.

❀ ❀ ❀

Lasso your "podner" and take him to a rodeo or square dance.

❀ ❀ ❀

Take a few tennis or golf lessons. Play a round or two of miniature golf.

❀ ❀ ❀

Put wheels on your heels and go roller skating.

❀ ❀ ❀

Rent a sailboat at the lake and enjoy the wind and waves for an afternoon.

❀ ❀ ❀

Feeling daring and adventuresome? How about a helicopter ride? bungee jumping? skydiving? Go white-water rafting and shoot big or little rapids.

❀ ❀ ❀

Take a self-defense course or karate lessons together.

❀ ❀ ❀

Close dancing is back. How about a few ballroom dance lessons to get your bodies swingin' and swayin'? Or get out your western gear and sneak away to kick up your heels at a honky-tonk, where nobody knows you.

❀ ❀ ❀

Ride the carousel or roller coaster at a carnival or fair. Try for a teddy bear by playing ring toss. Feast on cotton candy and crispy waffles.

❀ ❀ ❀

Ask for a remote booth in a romantic tea room. Sit on the same side. Blow out candles on the table. Or locate a quaint Italian restaurant where a strolling violinist can serenade you.

❀ ❀ ❀

Plan a progressive dinner or an international night of good food, with hors d'oeuvres at a Chinese restaurant, salad from the bar at a classy steak house, main course at a German eatery, dessert éclairs at a French pastry coffee shop. Here's a chance to try out those neat eating places your friends keep telling you about.

❀ ❀ ❀

Take a horse-drawn carriage ride through the park. Sneak a kiss and talk romantic.

❀ ❀ ❀

Stop somewhere along an unknown country road to pick up black walnuts. Climb to the top of a hill and be a cloud watcher. Pick wildflowers for drying.

❀ ❀ ❀

Go for an authentic steam train ride. Atlanta and some other cities offer a luxury steam train with elegant dining facilities to please any railroad buff.

❀ ❀ ❀

Curtain going up! Get tickets for a romantic theater presentation like *Phantom of the Opera* or *West Side Story*. Buy the tape to play at home later.

❀ ❀ ❀

Reserve tickets for anything—ballet, a jazz group, hockey, the symphony, speedway racing.

❀ ❀ ❀

The average human lifespan includes nearly four-thousand weekends! This week, you can challenge yourselves to spending under fifty dollars for your two-day getaway. Half the frugal fun will be getting your creative juices flowing figuring out ways to keep under budget.

Now, you have more money! You need ideas for great escapes that cost a bit more but just may be worth the months of penny-pinching you endured. Try these:

- Rent a motor coach, then tour national parks. Write for a brochure and stop at recommended Kamp-grounds of America.
- Ask your travel agent to locate an off-season Caribbean specialty cruise that offers whatever your interest is, maybe square dancing, inspirational speakers, baseball players. Two-for-one offers are common from April through mid-December.
- Book a leisurely barefoot Wind-jammer Cruise because you don't want social directors carrying loud whistles on your vacation. Bask in the sun on deck all day in shorts or swim-suit and on beautiful beaches at remote island stopovers. Yes, you really can help the crew sail the ship.
- Visit Hershey, Pennsylvania, choco-late factory of the world, for a sweet, sweet getaway or the resort at Cha-teau Elan in Braselton, Georgia, where wines are made next door. Tours of both are available.

❀ ❀ ❀

Need more ideas? Consider Vail or Vermont, Alabama or Antarctica. Visit a dude ranch, go horseback riding down the Grand Canyon, or meander down the Mississippi aboard a luxury paddlewheel boat. Write state tourist boards in the capital of each state or subscribe to *Romantic Hideaways* for sixty-five dollars a year: Barbara Brass Communications, P.O. Box 2340, Southampton, NY 11969.

The Traveler's Helper

You won't want to leave home without
some of these ideas

Earth's the right place for love:
I don't know where it's likely to go better.

ROBERT FROST, *Birches*

Let all the other couples complain and
whine about their spouse's job that keeps
them apart too much. Sure, it's tough
being separated, but you two are a crack
team of creativeness and are determined to
banish the blues despite the many miles
that sometimes separate. Right? You know
the good living the job provides, so you
can put together some savvy ideas to reach
out and touch one another over the miles.
If you are a quart or so low on know-how,
there are plenty of wonder-working suggestions here to supercharge your long-

211

distance relationship and keep your love affair alive and well. Out of sight doesn't mean out of mind. Your thoughts often turn toward your partner, so there are ways to let it be known.

IF HE TRAVELS A LOT IN HIS WORK

❀ ❀ ❀

Take the lug out of his luggage. Your traveling man will appreciate the time saved by your gift of a lightweight soft-sided carry-on suitcase with wheels and pull-out handle. It will roll easily, store in the overhead bin, and eliminate half-hour waits at airport baggage carousels. He won't want to leave home without your thoughtful gift that will remind him of you every time he heads out for faraway places.

❀ ❀ ❀

Fill the crevices and cracks of his suitcase with notes of encouragement or love or promises written on fancy stationery or heart shapes. Fold them in with the T-shirts, hide them inside sneakers and boxes of aspirin, inside socks, or in his wallet.

❀ ❀ ❀

Stick marriage enrichment books or tapes
in his suitcase. Be sure to include a mini
tape player.

❀ ❀ ❀

Make up a specialty cassette of carefully
chosen songs that he loves, maybe classic
oldies but goodies or gospel music. Or
compile a bunch of crazy comedy clips that
will bring out the giggles. One wife
included parts of a relaxation meditation
tape with quiet music and Scripture to
help her husband relax after a high-
pressure day. She added a personal message wishing him home safe and sound.

❀ ❀ ❀

Secretly pin a little snapshot of you and
the kids to his pajamas when you help him
pack.

❀ ❀ ❀

Stick in a note that says, "At eleven o'clock
each morning, I'll be thinking about you
and asking God's help, whatever you are
doing." When the clock strikes eleven, his

thoughts will probably turn to you, too.
Nice.

❀ ❀ ❀

Pack preaddressed postcards to you, the
kids, and maybe his parents. He can jot
down a bit of news to keep in touch each
day he's away without the hassle of shopping for cards and stamps or writing out
addresses.

❀ ❀ ❀

Pack a four-leaf clover with a message that
says, "Lucky me. I'm the one you always
come home to."

❀ ❀ ❀

Pack a night-light for him. It's a nice com-
fort when staying in strange places. He
won't stumble over the dressing table
stool on his way to the bathroom at
3:00 A.M..

❀ ❀ ❀

Gather up items for a snack pack so he
won't have to leave his hotel room (sometimes it's just not safe). When the midnight
cookie monster rears its ugly head, he will

bless you. Include boxed juices and other drinks.

❀ ❀ ❀

Send a greeting card, letter, or gift ahead to the hotel concierge (with tip) and ask to have it at the front desk so he can have mail when he arrives. Or have it placed on his pillow.

❀ ❀ ❀

Call to see if he arrived safely. Or you can be his morning wake-up call at 6:30, if you like. Better yet, on an extended trip, you could be there unexpectedly in person to wake him or perhaps be on hand to greet him as a surprise when he comes in at seven o'clock some evening.

❀ ❀ ❀

A huge "Welcome Home" banner strung up over the piano, dining-room door-way, or front entrance will let him know how glad you and the kids are to have him back home. Add crepe-paper streamers and fly a few balloons from the mailbox or tie yellow ribbons to a front-yard tree.

MAYBE IT'S *YOU* WHO DOES THE TRAVELING

Bet you miss each other a lot with all your comings and goings, don't you? The one who's traveling can show extra love and care, too.

❀ ❀ ❀

Leave him a blessing note:

The Lord bless thee, and keep thee:
The Lord make his face shine upon thee,
and be gracious unto thee:
The Lord lift up his countenance upon thee,
and give thee peace.

NUMBERS 6:24-26, KJV

❀ ❀ ❀

Leave behind personalized tapes where he is sure to find them. Maybe a good buddy would deliver his favorite supper by pre-arrangement.

❀ ❀ ❀

Send him a card every day you are away. Have envelopes addressed and stamped before leaving, in case you get busy. Or leave greeting cards on his dresser in envelopes marked Monday, Tuesday, Wednesday, etc, so he can open one per day. Stick silly stuff inside—Sweetarts, cinnamon gum, little lollipops, or licorice sticks. Maybe you can leave behind five daisies in a pretty vase on the kitchen table, one for each day you will be apart.

❀ ❀ ❀

Place a wrapped package (could it contain a terrific new underwear unmentionable and a photo of you wearing it?) on the bed. You have promised in an attached note to model your new outfit in person within forty-eight hours of your return home. Is there a matching piece for him?

❀ ❀ ❀

Prepare quarts of his favorite chili or soup for the freezer. For extra fun, leave behind mysterious foil-wrapped frozen packages of food as a surprise each night. He'll have everybody at work wondering what's for supper.

❀ ❀ ❀

Call him when you arrive. For that matter, call him every day or every hour if you two are into that sort of thing. Promise him something, even if it is only "I can't wait to tell you everything."

❀ ❀ ❀

Bring home souvenirs, little luxury bars of soap, bottles of expensive lotion, and luscious mints that hotel maids leave on the pillow. Shop in new or exotic stores for things he collects as a hobby or for new magazines he will enjoy that are not available at your local newsstand. It will be just like Christmas when you deliver the goods!

❀ ❀ ❀

Tell him you want him along on the next trip. Then save money and arrange it. Be sure it's one where you won't be quite so busy.

WHEN THE TWO OF YOU ARE FORTUNATE ENOUGH TO TRAVEL TOGETHER

❀ ❀ ❀

Pack a complete change of clothes for each of you in the other's suitcase. If one piece of luggage gets lost, there are clean clothes to wear while the airline locates the bag.

❀ ❀ ❀

Stop at bed-and-breakfasts if you can. There is something about these places that adds a note of romance even when you are traveling for business.

❑ From Mary: "With our lives at full speed seven days a week, it's hard to find time or baby-sitters for week-ends away. But I keep a 'just in case' bag packed and ready behind the hamper in the closet. I also have extra dollars saved and an emergency arrangement made with our sitter so if I call her at the last minute, she will be paid time and a half. No more hel-ter-skelter when my husband comes home every once in a while and says something like 'The boss's cabin in the mountains is available this week-end' or 'I've had enough. Let's call a halt to everything and go away some-place.' Sometimes these escapes are quiet, sometimes romantic, but they are always appreciated."

Resources for Reading

400 Creative Ways to Say I Love You by Alice Chapin (Tyndale House, 1995). Hundreds of creative ways to put married love into action. A long-term best-seller.

Always Daddy's Girl: Understanding Your Father's Impact on Who You Are by H. Norman Wright (Regal Books, 1981). Addresses the link between fathers and daughters, acknowledging that marriages often fail because of unresolved issues stemming from the wife's poor childhood relationship with her dad.

The Art of Understanding Your Mate by Dr. Cecil G. Osborne (Zondervan, 1988). Men and women are different. Their needs are different, as are the emotions that accompany those needs. The wonder is, Osborne points out, that there are so many successful marriages.

Courtship after Marriage by Zig Ziglar (Ballantine, 1992). Ziglar blends wisdom and humor with true examples to convince even born pessimists that romantic love can be rekindled even in the most distant marriage.

The Gift of Sex by Cliff and Joyce Penner (Word, 1991). A good instructional book that makes a difference if the couple will read it aloud together and proceed with the exercises.

Living, Loving and Learning by Leo Buscaglia (Fawcett, 1985). Buscaglia says, "I think loving persons must return to spontaneity—return to touching each other, holding each other, smiling at each other, thinking of each other, and caring about each other."

Love Must Be Tough by Dr. James Dobson (Word, 1983). Dobson discusses disrespect in marriage—infidelity, alcoholism, wife beating, emotional differences—and offers practical advice for the partner who wants desperately to hold things together. His principle of tough love is applicable not only to families in crisis but to healthy marriages as well.

The Marriage Builder by Dr. Lawrence Crabb (Zondervan, 1992). A blueprint for couples and counselors.

Marriage for a Lifetime by Floyd and Harriet Thatcher (Harold Shaw, 1995). What must married couples do to create a growing, healthy relationship? This book shares the responses and feelings of married couples.

Marriage Matters! by Stuart and Jill Briscoe (Harold Shaw, 1993). The Briscoes share a series of auto-biographical vignettes about their own courtship and marriage to encourage you to pull together when the challenges of career, family, schedules, or ministry try to pull you apart.

Men and Women, Enjoying the Difference by Dr. Lawrence Crabb (Zondervan, 1994). When they look at the world so differently, how can men and women ever hope to see eye to eye? Dr. Crabb explores those essential differences and makes them a source of enjoyment, not disagreement.

Stress Points in Marriage by Bill and Deana Blackburn (Waco, Tex., 1986). Learning to recognize stress and handle it creatively.

Strong Marriages, Secret Questions by Elizabeth Cody Newenhuyse (Lion Books, 1990). Explores the underlying doubts, questions, and fears that lie at the heart of even good marriages.

The Two Sides of Love by Gary Smalley and John Trent (Focus on the Family, 1992). Do you struggle to be firm and decisive—and sometimes say no—even when that's what you and your loved ones need? This book helps balance love's hard and soft sides every day.

About the Author

Alice Chapin does not consider herself an expert on love. Instead, she is an ardent collector of loving ideas for couples. She enjoys sharing hers with husband, Norman, a pastor-counselor, and learning his. Both claim to have been happily married (well, mostly!) for a long time. When do these two busy people find time to try some of these great ideas? Whenever they can! When asked by their four daughters *how many* they have tried, the Chapins just smile and wink at each other, so no one knows for sure! Alice and Norm live near Atlanta.

May the Lord make your love increase and overflow for each other.

THESSALONIANS 3:12